A BETTER PLACE

MILAN ALBERT

ISBN 978-1-63784-374-1 (paperback)
ISBN 978-1-63784-666-7 (digital)

Hawes & Jenkins Publishing
16427 N Scottsdale Road Suite 410
Scottsdale, AZ 85254
www.hawesjenkins.com

Printed in the United States of America

Paradox

Around love's exterior we gather alienated, indifferent, hung-over, and lonely... Bodies once warmed by emotional honesty now shiver in the doubt of their own experience...

Still, we laugh at faith and fidelity... Mere trinkets in a store window viewed with the scorn of a scrooge on Christmas eve...

Such a peculiar paradox we present... Faces pressed against the glass... All the while seeking warmth, yet forever playing it cool...

—Milan Albert

Contents

LET'S MAKE AMERICA GREAT AGAIN

Preface

The solutions and remedies contained herein are not suggestions or optional... They are absolutely necessary, or we lose freedom and liberty in the United States of America forever... And quite probably, we lose the United States of America itself...

For the entirety of civilization and the existence of this nation, workers have been subjugated into slavery to the bean counters... More and more, we are looked at as collateral on senseless debt and spending by the elites... We are thought of as nothing more than a bottomless piggy bank to fund the gluttony of elitist pigs... We are treated worse and worse by those with their thumbs pressing down upon us... King George's tyranny in 1760 was nothing compared to how we are now treated by the ruling class regressives (read carefully the Declaration of Independence, and you will see this truth to be self-evident) ... We are supposed to be tickled to joy if we have a job at all as they pocket 55 percent of the fruits of our labor... And you better like it or you will face great suffering and retribution... This has to stop...

For over one hundred years, regression has been allowed to go on unchecked... Regressives have manipulated the government, government agencies, the courts, the schools, the media, Hollywood, and everything else to the point where 20 percent of the population rules over the rest of us in absolute power and tyranny...

Elections in our republic have gotten to the point where it makes Russia look like Cub Scouts... Deadbeats and dead people voting regressive, voting machines rigged to change votes to regressive candidates, the IRS (and other agencies) used to suppress and silence any dissent and opposition to regression—all that has to stop...

A good friend of mine worked at a great company... At least it started out great... It was a mom-and-pop company set up as "employee owned" with stock options and profit sharing...

My friend wanted to earn a pension so his retirement wouldn't be just scrounging by on the tiny amount the social security Ponzi scam gives you...

Then a large corporation came along and bought that company... My friend told me if he would have known what was coming, he would have found other employment right then while he had time to earn a pension elsewhere... That corporation told all the workers, "We love the culture here, and we don't want to change a thing..."

Then they started changing everything...

Stock options were bought out at a fractional price... There was no more profit sharing... Christmas bonuses disappeared... Company parties turned into watching managers win all the prizes... Eventually, there were no company parties... Within a couple years, the front office management went from ten people to fifty people... Most of those people were not needed and only came up with one dumb ass idea after another... Most of these "managers" were indoctrinated regressives from academia...

The production line workers were the heart and soul of the company, and they were treated badly and not valued... Anyone conservative was discriminated against, and many were driven out and terminated without any misconduct... The irony in that was the conservatives were the best workers... Meanwhile, regressive workers who were slackers were promoted... And because of government stipends, half of the workforce was then refugees... Nine out of ten of those refugees were absolute slackers, knowing they would not be terminated because the government was paying the company to employ them... So, others had to do twice as much work to compensate...

My friend spent eleven years as lead man on one of the production lines at that company... His ideas and innovations that were implemented saved that company over three million dollars...

Then he was disrespected and demoted... He told me it got worse and worse to the point where he hated to go to work each day...

After giving seventeen of the best years of his life to the company, one day he was told his employment was being terminated (this came three days after he complained and raised concerns over the company violating OSHA regulations, illegally exposing workers to highly cancerous carcinogenic dust from chemical ingredients) ... There was no misconduct whatsoever involved, and when he asked them why he was being terminated, they wouldn't even give him a reason...

He was only a couple years from a full pension with full medical included... So, he was robbed of at least 350,000 dollars in pension and medical for being a conservative...

When that corporation bought that company, they were number 1 by far in their field... That corporation ran that company into the ground... They were passed by two competitors, and two years after my friend was terminated, that company went completely out of business...

This is a common result of anything nincompoop simpleton regressives do...

I study the writings of many highly intelligent and highly educated writers on many topics that are related to the contents herein...

It is good to get the insight and wisdom from such research, but at times, it can be a difficult reading... Sometimes, too much intricate detail can be like trying to read law books... All you end up with is a headache...

There's value in not taking the fun out of what should be easy... I will keep this simple as it should be...

Have a fun read...

May you always be blessed with happiness and good health...

Success

Success is a huge, important word...

Success has many meanings... In this endeavor, I hope to succeed in bringing the truth into light from the darkness and obscurity perpetuated by deception and misinformation from liberalism, socialism, and communism... All three are the same...just different stages of the same disease... much like opium, morphine, and heroin...

My greatest hope is to reach those who will, at first, read this and not want to believe it... But PLEASE persevere with an open mind and attitude, and perhaps you will come to the realization that you have been deceived and used and worse... I will delve into the tactics utilized by the left to perpetrate and disguise the lie of liberalism, and I will explain how the left has established the vehicles to carry on the indoctrination processes (always under the false guise of "for some collective good") ...

I will show in depth the playbook and methods that have been relentlessly in play in America for over one hundred years... Actually, over two hundred years when you see the root of the problem, which is global banking (global bankers use liberal leaders who, in turn, use those foolish enough to believe them) ... If you fight through the urge to resist this enlightenment, you will see how you have been deceived and controlled by purposeful misinformation and be able to break free and see the truth...

There is a clear, definite, and distinct difference between conservatism and liberalism... Conservatism always results in freedom, liberty, opportunity, prosperity, self-reliance, self-esteem, and hope for all... Liberalism always results in tyranny, financial ruin, and destitution...

The United States of America became the greatest nation to ever exist because of our founding principles, free market capitalism, and good deeds, foreign and domestic... There's a reason why the first choice of most people is to live in the USA (contrary perhaps to the left's misinformation that the USA is to blame for foreign and domestic wrongdoing) ... Our nation has done much more good than bad, far better than any nation ever... Our constitutional republic is a beacon of liberty, freedom, prosperity, opportunity, and hope to the rest of the world...

My father told me something profound when I was young, rebellious, and anti-establishment... He said, "Before you overthrow a government, you should have something better to replace it with..." So far, no one has come up with anything better than our constitutional republic… Certainly not any liberals, socialists, or communists…

But later I will outline a "better" government than even the founders established… Stay tuned…

Winston Churchill profoundly claimed that "spending your way out of a recession is like standing in a bucket and lifting yourself up…" Margaret Thatcher profoundly claimed that "the problem with socialism is that eventually you run out of other people's money…" Ronald Reagan also said some profound things… Not the least of which were that "liberalism is a disease" and "the truth is a stubborn thing…"

Stop and think about it… The truth is on the side of conservatism… Liberalism has to rely on lies… It can't be put simpler or more concise… Anytime there is a debate between conservatism and liberalism, the liberals can't focus on the facts and merits of the issue… Instead, they always try to keep repeating a lie, hoping that will eventually make it true, and they usually quickly resort to evasive tactics described by Herman Cain as shifting the subject, ignoring the facts, and name-calling… Just critically observe liberals in a debate and you will see this… If what I write herein strikes a nerve, the liberals won't be able to attack the facts so they will try to attack me on a personal level… We'll see how much the truth hurts… I hope a lot…

The other day, a survey of college students showed that they think they are the greatest generation... That was amazing to me... Those students have been indoctrinated by communist professors who deliberately did not teach them correct US history including the two greatest generations: our Founding Fathers' generation who freed us from tyranny and the WWII generation who did nothing less than save the world from tyranny...

I know how it is to be young and at a college student age... When we are young and impressionable, it's easy to be lured into whatever prevailing rebellious antiestablishment beliefs are popular (and subtly implanted by brainwash artists with concealed ulterior motives [i.e., to fool young people into being useful idiots—Joseph Stalin]) ... Not your fault, and there's no shame in coming to the realization that you have been tricked and used. I believe our nation is at a critical crossroad, and to survive as the greatest nation that ever existed, we need as many as possible to see through the lies, know the truth, and fight to save the greatest nation on earth from evil within... There's a lot of evil in the world, and those forces of evil are trying to get rid of the USA for a reason... Without the USA, they can do very bad things all over the world... And they would love nothing more than to do very bad things right here in the USA... Perhaps history will record a third greatest generation... I hope so...

I've thought long and hard and studied in depth the things that can and should be fixed in this country and will herein propose those solutions... Hope you enjoy reading further...

Outreach

There will be affirmation herein for those who see and know the truth... My goal is to do lots more than preach to the choir...

Because of the pain reflex included by the operant conditioning brainwash techniques of the Marxist left, this will not be as easy to read with an open mind by those who have been duped and victimized by that brainwashing... As you read on, there will be glimpses and examples of the brainwash, mass hypnosis, and dumbing down employed by the left...

I hope to reach those who are conservative and don't even realize it and those who have been restricted and confined in the darkness of deception... The light of truth is shining at the end of the tunnel...

I hope all liberal progressive (regressive) socialist Marxist democrats read this with an open mind full of critical thought, logic, reason, and common sense... I guarantee if that happens, many will wake up and be set free from the indoctrinated brain-washed hypnosis of liberal delirium madness...

I also guarantee that the braindead haters will hate... Attacks and false information smear tactics will be employed by liberal "fact-checkers" who stay up at night thinking of lies they hope you will believe... This will always come from those on the left who have a vested interest in liberalism (those who make their money and get their power from liberalism [e.g., Al Gore—man caused global warming hoax; Al Sharpton—race baiting; etc.]) ...

Keep in mind also that there are many on the right that are dumbed down and conditioned to the point where they automatically accept leftist narratives that have been allowed to permeate our culture and society because of lack of push back from the right...

All you really need to know is that there is a battle for the hearts and minds of the American people when there shouldn't be...

Conservatism shouldn't have to waste time and energy pushing back against dumb down tactics of liberalism... Instead, we should all be spending our time and energy promoting everyone to be the best they can be and achieve their greatest potential...

The left wants you to be constantly on the defense against flood after flood of destructive regressive policy issues that are intentionally designed to keep us in a defensive whack-a-mole posture...all the while keeping us from going on the offense against the more important regressive issues that would enable us to succeed in undoing regressive damage... The root of the problem is that regressives over time implement damage little by little (designed to be small enough to be accepted by people), and conservatives never push back and undo the damage done... Over the years, we find ourselves in a position where drastic measures are needed...

We should promote what made the American people and America great: knowledge, wisdom, individualism, independence, self-reliance, critical thought, logic, reason, common sense, opportunity, liberty, and freedom... The United States of America has done many more good things for this world than bad...much better than any other nation ever... Instead of teaching a false twisted liberal revised history of America to our children, we should be teaching them the truth and help them achieve the potential for greatness that is there inside them...

There's a reason why most people in the world want to live in and become a citizen of the United States of America... It's mostly freedom, liberty, and opportunity...

The United States of America's greatness and exceptionalism are embodied in our constitutional republic's founding principles of liberty, freedom, and limited government... Our Founding Fathers' wisdom is, to this day, pertinent and irreproachable... Soon herein will be included the Declaration of Independence, the constitution, and the bill of rights... Please read them slowly and carefully... Read them over and over with dedication to memory...

After the last sixty years of intense and subtle dumbing down, misinforming, brainwashing, and indoctrinating, it is often hard to get through to people who think they are liberals... I have a fishing buddy who believes he is a liberal... One day, we were fishing about thirty feet apart on the riverbank, and a conversation began about unions... (He is a union sheet metal worker and was complaining about not getting work and blaming Bush for the economy) ... In the Obama economy, it was hard to pay union workers twice as much as nonunion workers... I was trying to explain to him the difference between private sector unions (some of which when managed well are good and beneficial) and public sector unions (which should not exist) ... He spewed out some Marxist redistribution unicorn rainbow pixie dust hogwash and how it all had something to do with Bush lying so we could get all of Iraq's oil... Trying to keep up with his multiple tangents of subject-shifting, I told him Bush said something he believed was true... There's a difference between that and telling a deliberate lie (which Obama and his kind do every day)... I told him Saddam already used WMD on his own people and most likely moved them to Syria just prior to the invasion and that, besides, the best point of us invading Iraq was to get rid of an evil dictator and finally show a spine after years of Bill Clinton and his liberal yellow belly letting Al Qaeda get away with more and more and more until we ended up with 9/11... and I told him we haven't taken one drop of oil from Iraq... I also attempted to explain to him that this recession was not caused by Bush but by Clinton, Dodd, Franks, and the liberals when they created the Affordable Housing Act bill, which caused the subprime housing market bubble, which was the main catalyst of the recession... He looked at me and said, "Ya, but Cheney shot a guy..." I told him to try to focus... I tried to tell him that the Affordable Health Care bill was even worse than the Affordable Housing Act, and he looked at me and said, "Are you a racist?"

At that point, I told him he had a fish on and ended the conversation...

The bottom line is that you shouldn't trust and believe liberalism any further than you can throw a buffalo... What everyone should do first is to take a step back and question what anyone tries to get you to believe... Don't just blindly accept any assertion from anyone... There are also republican politicians who are not true conservatives and, in line with our founding principles, having the best interest of the American people...

If you always take a step back and question authority, you can see it for what it is... When liberal college professors try to indoctrinate, you have to see through it and not let them fill your head

with mush... Be very wary of professors who subtly try to teach you what to think instead of how to
think... When liberal media tries to misinform you
with propaganda spin, you have to recognize the lie
and not be brainwashed... When Marxist socialist
liberal politicians tell you they care about you and
want to do something "good" for you, disguising
their true intentions, don't let them turn you into a
"useful idiot..."

If you step back and pay close attention, you will
see liberals in Washington, the courts, Hollywood,
the media, and our schools are okie dokieing you
with lies, deception, spin, and misinformation...
You should be extremely insulted by them using
you and their lack of respect for your intelligence...

If you pay close attention for five minutes, it is
easy to see that liberal regressives are way too corrupt and dishonest to ever be believed and allowed
to be in charge of anything...

There is nothing good that has ever come from
regressive ideology and agenda... At the core of
regressive ideology is a lie because if the people
knew the truth, they would never be able to achieve
their goal of control... So, everything has to be a
deception dressed up to look good and sound good...
When you start from a lie, everything that follows is
not true...

The most evil-hearted and soulless of regressives are those who will look you in the eye and
lie on purpose... (And they have to lie on purpose

because they have to disguise their true intentions, or no one would elect them...) These are the regressives with a vested interest in liberalism (in other words, it is where they get their power and, thereby, their paychecks) ...

There's a regressive lady on Fox News... Her name is something like Shamu... She is a classic example of a regressive liar with a vested interest in liberal lies... (I think they have a direct telephone line to Ireland where they get their talking points from the Blarney Stone) ... If you watch Shamu when she's spewing her blithering idiocy, her eyes are constantly blinking... That tells you that she knows she is lying, and she does it anyway (to keep the deceived deceived) ...

There are many more in the vested category (most of which are mentally challenged...in other words, stupid, like Nancy Pelosi in congress and Debbie Wassermann-Schultz in the democrat party and many in the liberal media and many communist college professors and administrators in the department of education, which is the department of indoctrination...on your tax dollars) and know-nothing Hollywood regressive morons... All nincompoop simpleton blithering idiots...

As I will further explain in later chapters, millions in America have been purposely dumbed down for many years by these regressives so they can be deceived and used... There are millions of mass hypnotized believers in liberalism today who support these liars from whom they derive their power to destroy... It is these millions whom I hope will read this and see the light... The truth will set you free...

There is a struggle between good and evil that has been going on since time began... The best way to accurately describe this good and evil is conservative constitutional founding principle free market capitalism versus regressive liberal socialist communism... Freedom, liberty, and opportunity versus dictatorship, tyranny, and destitution...

Mook

Using the latest DNA technology, scientists have successfully traced genetics back to the very first liberal... He was a caveman named Mook... They called him Mook the Moocher... He believed he was smarter and knew better than everyone else how life should be... He thought he should be in charge and tell everyone else what to do... Meanwhile, he just wanted to lay around in the cave doing nothing while everyone else did the hunting and gathering... He thought everything should be his, and he would decide what he would allow all the others to have... Unfortunately, back then, the state of nature was survival of the fittest, and natural selection was the rule of the day... Nature did not select Mook, and he didn't last long...

No matter how advanced civilization becomes, the state of nature will always exist... The politically correct notions and narratives created by liberals are lies... Survival of the fittest trumps the myth that everyone "deserves" an equal outcome...

The natural instinct of humans is to do things the easiest way possible... Laziness and necessity are the mothers of invention...

Since the beginning of man, humans have been refining ways to get what others have... The honest ways are good and include getting your own or working for what you get from others (that's why private property was a big part of our founding principles) ...

As the millennia of man has transpired, many dubious and dishonest methods of taking from others have been refined... The earliest and most primitive forms are to take from others (steal) when they are not looking and unaware or to take by force... Today, we also have many forms of tyranny that accomplish this nefarious confiscation...

For over 130 years, we did not have income tax... We were free to keep all we earned and had the liberty to decide what our money would be spent on... Seems like today in America, there's a tax, fee, or fine for everything... And it seems the more money establishment agencies take, the more they squander frivolously...

Let's examine exactly how many taxes, fees, and fines we already actually pay...

Here is a partial list: accounts receivable tax, building permit tax, capital gains tax, CDL license tax, cigarette tax, corporate income tax, court fines (indirect taxes), deficit spending, dog license tax, federal income tax, federal unemployment tax

(FUTA), fishing license tax, fishing tags (indirect tax), hunting license tax, hunting tags (indirect tax), federal and state parks camping fees (indirect tax), national park use fees (indirect tax), state park use fees (indirect tax), food license tax, fuel permit tax, gasoline tax, inflation, inheritance tax interest expense (tax on the money), inventory tax, IRS interest charges (tax on top of tax), IRS penalties (tax on top of tax), liquor tax, local income tax, luxury taxes, marriage license tax, Medicare tax, property tax, real estate tax, septic permit tax, service charge taxes, social security tax, road usage taxes (truckers), sales taxes, recreational vehicle tax, road toll booth taxes, school tax, state income tax, state unemployment tax (SUTA), telephone federal excise tax, telephone federal, state, and local surcharge taxes, telephone minimum usage surcharge tax, telephone recurring and nonrecurring charges tax, telephone state and local tax, telephone usage charge tax, toll bridge taxes, toll tunnel taxes, parking fees and traffic fines (indirect taxation), trailer registration tax, utility taxes, vehicle registration tax, vehicle sales tax, watercraft registration tax, well permit tax, and workers compensation tax...

Whew...and the list goes on... Need I say more? Okay... I will...

There are over seventy-four thousand pages in our federal tax code alone...

With all of this, we are lucky to keep 40 percent of what we earn... The way we are paying taxes, fees, and fines makes the tyrannical taxation of colonial England that caused the Revolutionary War look small... And it certainly makes Mook the Moocher look like an inconsequential amateur...

The worst and most devastating tax of all is a hidden tax... It is inflation... This tax is levied not by representation but by manipulation... Inflation does more harm than we will probably ever realize...

Inflation comes primarily from failed fiscal policy coupled with globalist banking theft... It is the devaluation of the dollar... When you have fifty dollars and save fifty dollars, you then have one hundred dollars... but if inflation has devalued the dollar by 50 percent, you have gained nothing... But that other 50 percent went to someone... It did not just vanish... It went to those who control the money...

We have a federal reserve bank that does not belong to "we, the people..." It should never have been created... It was created by the first regressive president (Woodrow Wilson) in 1913 and has been the most destructive of all regressive blunders...

The federal reserve bank placed control of our economy in the hands of the extremely rich (many of whom are not even US citizens) ... This tool enables them to manipulate and profit as they wish (at the expense of our freedom, liberty, opportunity, prosperity, and well-being) ...

In six years under the regressive Obama regime, the federal reserve has printed three and one half trillion dollars out of thin air... This has been nothing less than devastating to the middle class... The direct result is the gap between the rich and the poor is wider than it has been since the 1920s...

The rich on Wall Street are making a killing at the expense of the middle class and the poor who are getting crushed... To put the stock market into proper and true perspective, the Dow would have to be at fifty thousand for the dollar to be worth what it was prerecession... That means filthy rich multi-billionaires are more than twice as rich, and "we, the people," are stupid to let them get away with it...

When those who control the money create inflation, it transfers the wealth you worked hard your whole life to achieve from your bank account into theirs... It is no different than taking everything your life stood for by force at gunpoint...

Since the first regressive, Mook the Moocher, man has relentlessly been refining the tactic of taking advantage of others...

After more than five thousand years of "civilization," the haves have the have nots enslaved in the rat race game...

The have nots risk life and limb commuting to and from work on the freeways every day, working themselves to the bone into an early grave...

It pains me to see this... People's life energy spent to keep governments and global bankers awash in riches...all the while many are trapped in debt payment, taxed excessively, devalued, and lucky to keep enough of their own money to have food on the table and maybe be able to take a yearly vacation...

The rat race is over, and the rats won...

This is the bigger issue that should and can be fixed...

For now, let's soon examine the last sixty years in America... There has been a harmful deliberate relentless regressive agenda going on while we were busy just trying to be happy and scratch two coins together...

Goodriddinsylvania

Secondhand breath of liberals is worse than secondhand smoke (not to mention secondhand chew) ...

Licking the lollipop of lunacy will turn you into a blithering idiot nincompoop simpleton...

Reagan once said liberalism is a disease... He was right... It is no different than alcohol... The more liberal Kool-Aid a person drinks, the more they become addicted to the sickness and can metaphorically and literally drink themselves to death... Only instead of destroying the liver, it destroys the brain...

What motivation could possibly be inside the minds of regressives?

What is it they think they are accomplishing by destroying everything that made America the greatest nation to ever exist?

What will be achieved when there are no more liberty, freedom, and opportunity and people in the world no longer want to come here?

What good will come from regressives controlling elected office and nonelected government agencies? The courts, the media, Hollywood, and public education?

When the news is not the truth but instead only lies the regressives want you to believe...when schools only focus on brainwashing young people to believe everything regressive and try to make sure they are dumbed down...when judges legislate from the bench, ignoring the constitution and rule of law...when movies and television shows are designed to promote regressive agendas...when elected regressives are dishonest and regressives in charge of federal, state, and local agencies persecute and prosecute everyone who does not obey and questions their honesty, what good will follow?

Seems like the end game of regressives is to regress back to the Dark Ages...a medieval existence where the serfs are all illiterate, uneducated, and destitute while the ruling royalty lives in luxury feasting and drinking fine wine...

This is why I refer to liberal commie democrats as regressives...

Liberalism must truly be a mental disorder to strive for such destruction...

No matter how they try to masquerade it as for some common "good," pulling on this or that fake heartstring, the regressive cause can only be truthfully described as evil...

For over two hundred years now, regressive policies have been shoved down the throats of the majority of Americans against their will, and we've had enough... Time to shove back... Time to undo every bit of the regressive tyranny and even put in safeguards so no one can ever use freedom and liberty to destroy our freedom and liberty ever again...

We need to create a new country called goodriddinsylvania (the farther away from America as possible) ... It can be like when Israel, Liberia, or many nations that have been created over the years... I would prefer it to be in Antarctica... But it can be anywhere appropriate... And by appropriate, I mean send all these communist regressives, bean counters, and their conspirators to some new country in the middle of the Middle East... Or perhaps make one country out of Honduras, El Salvador, and Guatemala... Wherever it is, call it goodriddinsylvania and let them figure out who's going to pay for everything...

This country is messed up... Those with no "skin in the game" should not be allowed to vote... If you don't pay taxes, you don't vote... If you are elected and you don't uphold and enforce the existing laws and constitution you swear to uphold that constitutes corruption, for that, you are automatically expatriated... You are no longer a citizen and never allowed to come here or apply for citizenship...

Power cannot be absolute on the federal level or any other level... Promising to give voters other people's money shall be punishable by expatriation... It is not in the interest of the well-being of America and the American people to have any politician tax the people, curry favor with voters by offering them back half that money in pork barrel projects and welfare, and squandering the other half of that money... That practice shall be automatic expatriation...

Beings how Mexico has relentlessly assaulted our southern border without regard for our sovereignty, it would also be fitting to take over the top three hundred miles of Mexico (although that would be too close for my liking), make a new country called goodriddinsylvania, build and guard an impenetrable wall on our southern border, and send all regressives, their career welfare supporters, the bean counters, and the illegal aliens to goodriddinsylvania... Allow them thirty thousand dollars each or 10 percent of their wealth (whichever is greater, except illegal aliens), wish them well, and tell them to never come back or they will be arrested on sight.

The biggest threat to the regressive agenda is intelligent well educated informed knowledgeable voters.

There are many liberals/regressives that are good hearted well-meaning people.

They have been deceived and their good nature taken advantage of by well refined fancy feel good rhetoric from the communist fascist regressive left whose livelihood comes from this lying and deceiving.

Many of the good-hearted liberals that have been tricked into believing the lies of the left can be eventually cured and saved.

The biggest obstacle to this is that it is easier to fool someone than to convince them they have been fooled. Most of the followers of David Koresh and Jim Jones were so caught up in the mass hypnosis that instead of accepting their mistake they chose to burn to death and die drinking poison. A certain percentage of regressives will be that extreme.

The biggest positives to this end are that the truth is a stubborn thing and the good-hearted people are not stupid (even though the left believes they are and counts on them being stupid). That is why the left took over the education system to try to ensure that the masses are dumbed down enough to be fooled. That's why so many high school graduates today know less than I knew in junior high. And so many college students today would not even qualify to graduate high school fifty years ago.

With JFK's "affirmative action" LBJ's federal monetary takeover of education, and Carter's creation of the Department of Education the dye was cast to control curriculum and teach (or not teach) whatever the regressives wanted.

The Democrat Party, the media, our schools, Hollywood, Department of Energy, EPA, IRS, etc. have been taken over by absolutely insane fascist Marxists.

Our school curriculum has been taken over by regressives. The potential for greatness in too many has been stolen by government dependency on welfare.

People used to come to America for freedom, liberty, prosperity, and opportunity. Now many want to come here to freeload.

That attracts the wrong people. Our wealth, well-being, and culture has been diminished by the regressive agenda assaults.

So now it's hard to count the freedoms and liberties lost and we find ourselves neck deep in a police/welfare state.

40 Percent

I look around on the roads in America and notice that 40 percent of the vehicles are foreign made... I can't help but wonder what's the correlation between that, and in the US, every middle- and lower-class person is losing 40 percent of their life savings and home values in this current intentionally created recession... There is a direct and definite correlation...

In the early sixties, I went to the auto plants in Detroit... I remember thousands of acres of parking lots filled with brand-new cars lined up, waiting to be shipped throughout the country. Detroit was a booming and thriving great American city. Two million proud hard-working Americans. Now anyone that had the means has left there and maybe 600,000 people are left in Detroit. Many of them are to some degree destitute and have been unable to leave. The housing market in Detroit is so bad you can't give away houses. This was not natural or necessary. And it was not by happenstance.

Regressive ideology created the decline of Detroit and the American Auto Industry.

In the 70's there was a deliberate misinformation disinformation campaign launched that perpetrated the myth that foreign vehicles were made better and cheaper than American made automobiles. This was never true but was repeated over and over until the gullible masses were dumbed down. So, we gave away part of our greatness and have been supporting foreign economies ever since.

It started with a few Datsun mini pickups. And now we have Honda's, Toyota's, Nissan's, Mitsubishi's, and countless others. Some say, "well they are made here". That's a hogwash talking point argument. The company profits still go to those foreign economies.

So, in retrospect, what was the true cost of buying all those foreign vehicles?

*(We have to stop doing business in China. And we have to not allow China to own property in the United States. It is enabling China to build a strong military to one day use against us.) *

The whole time this shift to supporting foreign economies was going on many other subtle hidden regressive agendas were taking place, while we were not paying attention.

Can you imagine someone from the 50's waking up at this time? All the freedoms and liberties from then are now gone, eroded away, tiny bit by bit.

While we were busy working our tails off 24/7 trying to "get by", raise children and watching our favorite television shows, the regressive agenda was incessantly going on.

Even in our favorite television shows (and commercials) there was subliminal regressive agenda and social engineering propaganda.

(Have you noticed there is more commercial time now a days than program time? There used to be 2 minutes of commercial time every 15 minutes.) Now there are 5-6 minutes of commercials to every 10 minutes of programming. We are more and more being seen as easily duped fools that need to be parted from our money. And the government sees us more and more the same way.)

All through the 70's there was a racist emphasis on blacks. This set up the relentless use of the race card later. Not to mention the undoing of Martin Luther King Jr's dream via the race baiting industry. (All aimed at the end game to keep blacks voting democrat).

There was a disproportionate amount of black programming. A few examples are Sister Sister, Family Matters, The Jamie Foxx show, the Steve Harvey show, Sanford and Son, Hanging with Me, Cooper, Different Strokes, Roe, The Parent Hood, Moesha, 227, What's Happening, Fat Albert, and the Cosby kids, Living Single and The Jeffersons, Martin, Good Times, A Different World, The Fresh

Prince of Bel Air, and The Cosby Show (to name a few).

All through the 80's there was a heavy emphasis on females. (for the purpose of herding females into voting democrat via the gender card) As the hero, the lead role or the one in charge there was social engineering all over the boob tube. All geared to found and reinforce the female grievance industry. A few examples are Wonder Woman, Cagney & Lacey, Sky Runner, Alice, Designing Women, Flo, Golden Girls, Kate & Allie, She's the Sherrif, Sister Kate, Valerie etc. and many movies with the same themes.

All through the 90's we were subjected (conditioned/indoctrinated) to the gay agenda in the same way, so it could be used whenever convenient to regression. If you watch television and the media, you will think that over half the population is gay.

I haven't watched much "entertainment television since 2000... I guess I got tired of my intelligence being insulted.

The whole time we were being pre-conditioned to accept the black, female, and gay agendas, we were also being inundated with police shows. This was pre-conditioning for the ever over-reaching "police state".

I remember when you didn't need to lock your doors (like the prison society has now become).

Neighbors used to watch out for their neighbors. Then for an ulterior reason, they started

"Neighborhood Watch" Next thing you know they had McGruff the crime dog, taking a bite out of freedom and liberty.

So, they conditioned people into accepting the concept of everyone spying on each other. Now we have liberals everywhere watching everyone's every move. Never mind the obsolete concept of "mind your own business".

And now we have fully militarized combat ready agencies like the BLM. Not to mention police forces with cart blanch authorities over our privacy and private property. (And now we have three FBI assassins posing as Oregon State Troopers, murdering Lavoy Finicum, while his hands are in the air and then planting a gun on him to tell the lie that he was reaching for a gun, and they are allowed to get away with it.)

A similar hijack agenda happened when we came out against littering and started Earth Day. It began to just clean up the roads and public areas. Next thing you know we had environmental fascists everywhere acting like trees are not a renewable resource and claiming the end is near because of global cooling. Another Ice age was on the way. That didn't work out so now it has morphed into Global warming. It never ends with these regressives. And none of it is about concerns for the environment. It is about control and power.

This is the same as the Marxist goal of banning guns. The left will twist every situation they can into an excuse to attack the 2nd amendment. But it is never about the concern for our safety like they claim, or they wouldn't be bringing thin skinned Muslim terrorists here as fast as they can by the boat loads. It is about achieving absolute tyranny... and without regard for how many Americans die at their hands.

In the 80's I first noticed a huge shift in our culture. I saw more and more professional unwed mothers. These were females with no interest in getting married. But they made sure to get pregnant every two years so they could receive a welfare check and food stamps in perpetuity Never mind who the fathers were.

Now we have prisons full of those fatherless children.

Thanks to regressive social engineering like JFK's affirmative action and LBJ's "great society" and "war on poverty" we have more black, white, and brown slaves trapped in inner city plantations in worse poverty and destitution than we ever would have had without that engineering.

Of course, it was on purpose and did not have the best interest of those "slaves" and this country in mind.

It has always been about power and control of our money.

We had plenty of roads, railroads, schools, freedom, liberty, opportunity, and prosperity before Woodrow Wilson came along and started the methodical destruction of what made this country great. And any poor and needy people were taken care of just fine by churches and charities.

Also, thanks to LBJ injecting "blackmail money" into education and Jimmy Carter creating the Department of Education we now have Generations X, Y and Z that have been raised by regressives. They were taught what to think instead of how to think. They have been taught that America is bad and is to blame. Many of the younger people in our country today were raised on lies. They were not taught the greatness and great promise of this country. This is confirmed in the truth that people from everywhere in the world want to come here.

*(Strange how the Federal government takes money from the states, then threatens to withhold those states own money from them if they don't comply with federal mandates, Figure that one out. Most things should be left in the states to begin with, In fact, the Constitution calls for most things to be left to the states.)

Declaration of Independence

The Declaration of Independence, Constitution, and Bill of Rights are timeless documents reflecting our founding principles... Please read and let the light of truth set you free.

Woodrow Wilson first coined the phrase "living document" in 1913 referring to the Constitution and Bill of Rights to infer that they can be changed on a whim and that they can evolve. Since then, regressives, have gone ape crazy trying to change those documents (when convenient to their agendas) to achieve power and control and destroy the freedom and liberty mandated in those documents. But the Constitution and Bill of Rights are "carved in stone" and not "living documents" to be interpreted as saying anything other than what they say.

The unanimous Declaration of the thirteen United States of America

When in the Course of human events, it becomes necessary for one people to dissolve the political bands which have connected them with another, and to assume among the powers of the earth, the separate and equal station to which the Laws of Nature and of Nature's God entitle them, a decent respect to the opinions of mankind requires that they should declare the causes which impel them to the separation.

We hold these truths to be self-evident, that all men are created equal, that they are endowed by their Creator with certain unalienable Rights, that among these are Life, Liberty and the pursuit of Happiness.--That to secure these rights, Governments are instituted among Men, deriving their just powers from the consent of the governed, --That whenever any Form of Government becomes destructive of these ends, it is the Right of the People to alter or to abolish it, and to institute new Government, laying its foundation on such principles and organizing its powers in such form, as to them shall seem most likely to effect their Safety and Happiness. Prudence, indeed, will dictate that Governments long established should not be changed for light and transient causes; and accordingly all experience hath shewn, that mankind are more disposed to suffer, while evils are sufferable, than to right themselves by abolishing the forms to which they are accustomed. But when a long train of abuses and usurpations, pursuing invariably the same Object evinces a design to reduce them under absolute Despotism, it is their right, it is their duty, to throw off such Government, and to provide new Guards for their future security.--Such has been the patient sufferance of these Colonies; and such is now the necessity which constrains them to alter their former Systems of Government. The history of the present King of Great Britain is a history of repeated injuries and usurpations, all having in direct object the establishment of an absolute Tyranny over these States. To prove this, let Facts be submitted to a candid world.

He has refused his Assent to Laws, the most wholesome and necessary for the public good.

He has forbidden his Governors to pass Laws of immediate and pressing importance, unless suspended in their operation till his Assent should be obtained; and when so suspended, he has utterly neglected to attend to them.

He has refused to pass other Laws for the accommodation of large districts of people, unless those people would relinquish the right of Representation in the Legislature, a right inestimable to them and formidable to tyrants only.

He has called together legislative bodies at places unusual, uncomfortable, and distant from the depository of their public Records, for the sole purpose of fatiguing them into compliance with his measures.

He has dissolved Representative Houses repeatedly, for opposing with manly firmness his invasions on the rights of the people.

He has refused for a long time, after such dissolutions, to cause others to be elected; whereby the Legislative powers, incapable of Annihilation, have returned to the People at large for their exercise; the State remaining in the mean time exposed to all the dangers of invasion from without, and convulsions within.

He has endeavoured to prevent the population of these States; for that purpose obstructing the Laws for Naturalization of Foreigners; refusing to pass others to encourage their migrations hither, and raising the conditions of new Appropriations of Lands.

He has obstructed the Administration of Justice, by refusing his Assent to Laws for establishing Judiciary powers.

He has made Judges dependent on his Will alone, for the tenure of their offices, and the amount and payment of their salaries.

He has erected a multitude of New Offices, and sent hither swarms of Officers to harrass our people, and eat out their substance.

He has kept among us, in times of peace, Standing Armies without the Consent of our legislatures.

He has affected to render the Military independent of and superior to the Civil power.

He has combined with others to subject us to a jurisdiction foreign to our constitution, and unacknowledged by our laws; giving his Assent to their Acts of pretended Legislation:

For Quartering large bodies of armed troops among us:

For protecting them, by a mock Trial, from punishment for any Murders which they should commit on the Inhabitants of these States:

For cutting off our Trade with all parts of the world:

For imposing Taxes on us without our Consent:

For depriving us in many cases, of the benefits of Trial by Jury:

For transporting us beyond Seas to be tried for pretended offences

For abolishing the free System of English Laws in a neighbouring Province, establishing therein an Arbitrary government, and enlarging its Boundaries so as to render it at once an example and fit instrument for introducing the same absolute rule into these Colonies:

For taking away our Charters, abolishing our most valuable Laws, and altering fundamentally the Forms of our Governments:

For suspending our own Legislatures, and declaring themselves invested with power to legislate for us in all cases whatsoever.

He has abdicated Government here, by declaring us out of his Protection and waging War against us.

He has plundered our seas, ravaged our Coasts, burnt our towns, and destroyed the lives of our people.

He is at this time transporting large Armies of foreign Mercenaries to compleat the works of death, desolation and tyranny, already begun with circumstances of Cruelty & perfidy scarcely paralleled in the most barbarous ages, and totally unworthy the Head of a civilized nation.

He has constrained our fellow Citizens taken Captive on the high Seas to bear Arms against their Country, to become the executioners of their friends and Brethren, or to fall themselves by their Hands.

He has excited domestic insurrections amongst us, and has endeavoured to bring on the inhabitants of our frontiers, the merciless Indian Savages, whose known rule of warfare, is an undistinguished destruction of all ages, sexes and conditions.

In every stage of these Oppressions We have Petitioned for Redress in the most humble terms: Our repeated Petitions have been answered only by repeated injury. A Prince whose character is thus marked by every act which may define a Tyrant, is unfit to be the ruler of a free people.

Nor have We been wanting in attentions to our Brittish brethren. We have warned them from time to time of attempts by their legislature to extend an unwarrantable jurisdiction over us. We have reminded them of the circumstances of our emigration and settlement here. We have appealed to their native justice and magnanimity, and we have conjured them by the ties of our common kindred to disavow these usurpations, which, would inevitably interrupt our connections and correspondence. They too have been deaf to the voice of justice and of consanguinity. We must, therefore, acquiesce in the necessity, which denounces our Separation, and hold them, as we hold the rest of mankind, Enemies in War, in Peace Friends.

We, therefore, the Representatives of the united States of America, in General Congress, Assembled, appealing to the Supreme Judge of the world for the rectitude of our intentions, do, in the Name, and by Authority of the good People of these Colonies, solemnly publish and declare, That these United Colonies are, and of Right ought to be Free and Independent States; that they are Absolved from all Allegiance to the British Crown, and that all political connection between them and the State of Great Britain, is and ought to be totally dissolved; and that as Free and Independent States, they have full Power to levy War, conclude Peace, contract Alliances, establish Commerce, and to do all other Acts and Things which Independent States may of right do. And for the support of this Declaration, with a firm reliance on the protection of divine Providence, we mutually pledge to each other our Lives, our Fortunes and our sacred Honor.

Georgia
Button Gwinnett
Lyman Hall
George Walton

North Carolina
William Hooper
Joseph Hewes
John Penn

South Carolina
Edward Rutledge
Thomas Heyward, Jr.
Thomas Lynch, Jr.
Arthur Middleton

Massachusetts
John Hancock

Maryland
Samuel Chase
William Paca
Thomas Stone
Charles Carroll of Carrollton

Virginia
George Wythe
Richard Henry Lee
Thomas Jefferson
Benjamin Harrison
Thomas Nelson, Jr.
Francis Lightfoot Lee
Carter Braxton

Pennsylvania
Robert Morris
Benjamin Rush
Benjamin Franklin
John Morton
George Clymer
James Smith
George Taylor
James Wilson
George Ross

Delaware
Caesar Rodney
George Read
Thomas McKean

New York
William Floyd
Philip Livingston
Francis Lewis
Lewis Morris

New Jersey
Richard Stockton
John Witherspoon
Francis Hopkinson
John Hart
Abraham Clark

New Hampshire
Josiah Bartlett
William Whipple

Massachusetts
Samuel Adams
John Adams
Robert Treat Paine
Elbridge Gerry

Rhode Island
Stephen Hopkins
William Ellery

Connecticut
Roger Sherman
Samuel Huntington
William Williams
Oliver Wolcott

New Hampshire
Matthew Thornton

The Constitution

We the People of the United States, in Order to form a more perfect Union, establish Justice, ensure domestic Tranquility, provide for the common defense, promote the general Welfare, and secure the Blessings of Liberty to ourselves and our Posterity, do ordain and establish this Constitution for the United States of America.

ARTICLE. I.

Section. 1.

All legislative Powers herein granted shall be vested in a Congress of the United States, which shall consist of a Senate and House of Representatives.

Section. 2.

The House of Representatives shall be composed of Members chosen every second Year by the People of the several States, and the Electors in each State shall have the Qualifications requisite for Electors of the most numerous Branch of the State Legislature.

No Person shall be a Representative who shall not have attained to the Age of twenty five Years, and been seven Years a Citizen of the United States, and who shall not, when elected, be an Inhabitant of that State in which he shall be chosen.

Representatives and direct Taxes shall be apportioned among the several States which may be included within this Union, according to their respective Numbers, which shall be determined by adding to the whole Number of free Persons, including those bound to Service for a Term of Years, and excluding Indians not taxed, three fifths of all other Persons. The actual Enumeration shall be made within three Years after the first Meeting of the Congress of the United States, and within every subsequent Term of ten Years, in such Manner as they shall by Law direct. The Number of Representatives shall not exceed one for every thirty Thousand, but each State shall have at Least one Representative; and until such enumeration shall be made, the State of New Hampshire shall be entitled to choose three, Massachusetts eight, Rhode-Island and Providence Plantations one, Connecticut five, New-York six, New Jersey four, Pennsylvania eight, Delaware one, Maryland six, Virginia ten, North Carolina five, South Carolina five, and Georgia three.

When vacancies happen in the Representation from any State, the Executive Authority thereof shall issue Writs of Election to fill such Vacancies.

The House of Representatives shall choose their Speaker and other Officers; and shall have the sole Power of Impeachment.

Section. 3.

The Senate of the United States shall be composed of two Senators from each State, chosen by the Legislature thereof, for six Years; and each Senator shall have one Vote.

Immediately after they shall be assembled in Consequence of the first Election, they shall be divided as equally as may be into three Classes. The Seats of the Senators of the first Class shall be vacated at the Expiration of the second Year, of the second Class at the Expiration of the fourth Year, and of the third Class at the Expiration of the sixth Year, so that one third may be chosen every second Year; and if Vacancies happen by Resignation, or otherwise, during the Recess of the Legislature of any State, the Executive thereof may make temporary Appointments until the next Meeting of the Legislature, which shall then fill such Vacancies.

No Person shall be a Senator who shall not have attained to the Age of thirty Years and been nine Years a Citizen of the United States, and who shall not, when elected, be an Inhabitant of that State for which he shall be chosen.

The Vice President of the United States shall be President of the Senate, but shall have no Vote, unless they be equally divided.

The Senate shall chuse their other Officers, and also a President pro tempore, in the Absence of the Vice President, or when he shall exercise the Office of President of the United States.

The Senate shall have the sole Power to try all Impeachments. When sitting for that Purpose, they shall be on Oath or Affirmation. When the President of the United States is tried, the Chief Justice shall preside: And no Person shall be convicted without the Concurrence of two thirds of the Members present.

Judgment in Cases of Impeachment shall not extend further than to removal from Office, and disqualification to hold and enjoy any Office of honor, Trust, or Profit under the United States: but the Party convicted shall nevertheless be liable and subject to Indictment, Trial, Judgment and Punishment, according to Law.

Section. 4.

The Times, Places and Manner of holding Elections for Senators and Representatives, shall be prescribed in each State by the Legislature thereof; but the Congress may at any time by Law make or alter such Regulations, except as to the Places of choosing Senators.

The Congress shall assemble at least once in every Year, and such Meeting shall be on the first Monday in December, unless they shall by Law appoint a different Day.

Section. 5.

Each House shall be the Judge of the Elections, Returns and Qualifications of its own Members, and a Majority of each shall constitute a Quorum to do Business; but a smaller Number may adjourn from day to day, and may be authorized to compel the Attendance of absent Members, in such Manner, and under such Penalties as each House may provide.

Each House may determine the Rules of its Proceedings, punish its members for disorderly Behavior, and, with the Concurrence of two thirds, expel a member.

Each House shall keep a Journal of its Proceedings, and from time to time publish the same, excepting such Parts as may in their Judgment require Secrecy; and the Yeas and Nays of the Members of either House on any question shall, at the Desire of one fifth of those Present, be entered on the Journal.

Neither House, during the Session of Congress, shall, without the Consent of the other, adjourn for more than three days, nor to any other Place than that in which the two Houses shall be sitting.

Section. 6.

The Senators and Representatives shall receive a Compensation for their Services, to be ascertained by Law, and paid out of the Treasury of the United States. They shall in all Cases, except Treason, Felony and Breach of the Peace, be privileged from Arrest during their Attendance at the Session of their respective Houses, and in going to and returning from the same; and for any Speech or Debate in either House, they shall not be questioned in any other Place.

No Senator or Representative shall, during the Time for which he was elected, be appointed to any civil Office under the Authority of the United States, which shall have been created, or the Emoluments whereof shall have been increased during such time; and no Person holding any Office under the United States, shall be a Member of either House during his Continuance in Office.

Section. 7.

All Bills for raising Revenue shall originate in the House of Representatives; but the Senate may propose or concur with Amendments as on other Bills.

Every Bill which shall have passed the House of Representatives and the Senate, shall, before it become a Law, be presented to the President of the United States; If he approve he shall sign it, but if not he shall return it, with his Objections to that House in which it shall have originated, who shall enter the Objections at large on their Journal, and proceed to reconsider it. If after such Reconsideration two thirds of that House shall agree to pass the Bill, it shall be sent, together with the Objections, to the other House, by which it shall likewise be reconsidered, and if approved by two thirds of that House, it shall become a Law. But in all such Cases the Votes of both Houses shall be determined by yeas and Nays, and the Names of the Persons voting for and against the Bill shall be entered on the Journal of each House respectively. If any Bill shall not be returned by the President within ten Days (Sundays excepted) after it shall have been presented to him, the Same shall be a Law, in like Manner as if he had signed it, unless the Congress by their Adjournment prevent its Return, in which Case it shall not be a Law.

Every Order, Resolution, or Vote to which the Concurrence of the Senate and House of Representatives may be necessary (except on a question of Adjournment) shall be presented to the President of the United States; and before the Same shall take Effect, shall be approved by him, or being disapproved by him, shall be repassed by two thirds of the Senate and House of Representatives, according to the Rules and Limitations prescribed in the Case of a Bill.

Section. 8.

The Congress shall have Power To lay and collect Taxes, Duties, Imposts and Excises, to pay the Debts and provide for the common Defense and general Welfare of the United States; but all Duties, Imposts and Excises shall be uniform throughout the United States.

To borrow Money on the credit of the United States.

To regulate Commerce with foreign Nations, and among the several States, and with the Indian Tribes.

To establish a uniform Rule of Naturalization, and uniform Laws on the subject of Bankruptcies throughout the United States.

To coin Money, regulate the Value thereof, and of foreign Coin, and fix the Standard of Weights and Measures.

To provide for the Punishment of counterfeiting the Securities and current Coin of the United States.

To establish Post Offices and post Roads.

To promote the Progress of Science and useful Arts, by securing for limited Times to Authors and

Inventors the exclusive Right to their respective Writings and Discoveries.

To constitute Tribunals inferior to the supreme Court.

To define and punish Piracies and Felonies committed on the high Seas, and Offences against the Law of Nations.

To declare War, grant Letters of Marque and Reprisal, and make Rules concerning Captures on Land and Water.

To raise and support Armies, but no Appropriation of Money to that Use shall be for a longer Term than two Years.

To provide and maintain a Navy.

To make Rules for the Government and Regulation of the land and naval Forces.

To provide for calling forth the Militia to execute the Laws of the Union, suppress Insurrections and repel Invasions.

To provide for organizing, arming, and disciplining, the Militia, and for governing such Part of them as may be employed in the Service of the United States, reserving to the States respectively, the Appointment of the Officers, and the Authority of training the Militia according to the discipline prescribed by Congress.

To exercise exclusive Legislation in all Cases whatsoever, over such District (not exceeding ten Miles square) as may, by Cession of particular States, and the Acceptance of Congress, become the

Seat of the Government of the United States, and to exercise like Authority over all Places purchased by the Consent of the Legislature of the State in which the Same shall be, for the Erection of Forts, Magazines, Arsenals, dock-Yards, and other needful Buildings;—And

To make all Laws which shall be necessary and proper for carrying into Execution the foregoing Powers, and all other Powers vested by this Constitution in the Government of the United States, or in any Department or Officer thereof.

Section. 9.

The Migration or Importation of such Persons as any of the States now existing shall think proper to admit, shall not be prohibited by the Congress prior to the Year one thousand eight hundred and eight, but a Tax or duty may be imposed on such Importation, not exceeding ten dollars for each Person.

The Privilege of the Writ of Habeas Corpus shall not be suspended, unless in Cases of Rebellion or Invasion the public Safety may require it.

No Bill of Attainder or ex post facto Law shall be passed.

No Capitation, or other direct, Tax shall be laid, unless in Proportion to the Census or enumeration herein before directed to be taken.

No Tax or Duty shall be laid on Articles exported from any State.

No Preference shall be given by any Regulation of Commerce or Revenue to the Ports of one State over those of another: nor shall Vessels bound to, or from, one State, be obliged to enter, clear, or pay Duties in another.

No Money shall be drawn from the Treasury, but in Consequence of Appropriations made by Law; and a regular Statement and Account of the Receipts and Expenditures of all public Money shall be published from time to time.

No Title of Nobility shall be granted by the United States: And no Person holding any Office of Profit or Trust under them, shall, without the Consent of the Congress, accept of any present, Emolument, Office, or Title, of any kind whatever, from any King, Prince, or foreign State.

Section. 10.

No State shall enter into any Treaty, Alliance, or Confederation; grant Letters of Marque and Reprisal; coin Money; emit Bills of Credit; make any Thing but gold and silver Coin a Tender in Payment of Debts; pass any Bill of Attainder, ex post facto Law, or Law impairing the Obligation of Contracts, or grant any Title of Nobility.

No State shall, without the Consent of the Congress, lay any Imposts or Duties on Imports or Exports, except what may be absolutely necessary for executing it's inspection Laws: and the net Produce of all Duties and Imposts, laid by any State on Imports or Exports, shall be for the Use of the Treasury of the United States; and all such Laws shall be subject to the Revision and Controul of the Congress.

No State shall, without the Consent of Congress, lay any Duty of Tonnage, keep Troops, or Ships of War in time of Peace, enter into any Agreement or Compact with another State, or with a foreign Power, or engage in War, unless actually invaded, or in such imminent Danger as will not admit of delay.

ARTICLE. II.

Section. 1.

The executive Power shall be vested in a President of the United States of America. He shall hold his Office during the Term of four Years, and, together with the Vice President, chosen for the same Term, be elected, as follows.

Each State shall appoint, in such Manner as the Legislature thereof may direct, a Number of Electors, equal to the whole Number of Senators and Representatives to which the State may be entitled in the Congress: but no Senator or Representative, or Person holding an Office of Trust or Profit under the United States, shall be appointed an Elector.

The Electors shall meet in their respective States, and vote by Ballot for two Persons, of whom one at least shall not be an Inhabitant of the same State with themselves. And they shall make a List of all the Persons voted for, and of the Number of Votes for each, which List they shall sign and certify, and transmit sealed to the Seat of the Government of the United States, directed to the President of the Senate. The President of the Senate shall, in the Presence of the Senate and House of Representatives, open all the Certificates, and the Votes shall then be counted. The Person having the greatest Number of Votes shall be the President, if such Number be a Majority of the whole Number of Electors appointed; and if there be more than one who have such Majority, and have an equal Number of Votes, then the House of Representatives shall immediately chuse by Ballot one of them for President; and if no Person have a Majority, then from the five highest on the List the said House shall in like Manner chuse the President. But in chusing the President, the Votes shall be taken by States, the Representation from each State having one Vote; A quorum for this Purpose shall consist of a Member or Members from two thirds of the States, and a Majority of all the States shall be necessary to a Choice. In every Case, after the Choice of the President, the Person having the greatest Number of Votes of the Electors shall be the Vice President. But if there should remain two or more who have equal Votes, the Senate shall choose from them by Ballot the Vice President.

The Congress may determine the Time of choosing the Electors, and the Day on which they shall give their Votes, which Day shall be the same throughout the United States.

No Person except a natural born Citizen, or a Citizen of the United States, at the time of the Adoption of this Constitution, shall be eligible to the Office of President; neither shall any Person be eligible to that Office who shall not have attained to the Age of thirty-five Years, and been fourteen Years a Resident within the United States.

In Case of the Removal of the President from Office, or of his Death, Resignation, or Inability to discharge the Powers and Duties of the said Office, the Same shall devolve on the Vice President, and the Congress may by Law provide for the Case of Removal, Death, Resignation or Inability, both of the President and Vice President, declaring what Officer shall then act as President, and such Officer shall act accordingly, until the Disability be removed, or a President shall be elected.

The President shall, at stated Times, receive for his Services, a Compensation, which shall neither be increased nor diminished during the Period for which he shall have been elected, and he shall not receive within that Period any other Emolument from the United States, or any of them.

Before he enters on the Execution of his Office, he shall take the following Oath or Affirmation: — "I do solemnly swear (or affirm) that I will faithfully execute the Office of President of the United States, and will to the best of my Ability, preserve, protect and defend the Constitution of the United States."

Section. 2.

The President shall be Commander in Chief of the Army and Navy of the United States, and of the Militia of the several States, when called into the actual Service of the United States; he may require the Opinion, in writing, of the principal Officer in each of the executive Departments, upon any Subject relating to the Duties of their respective Offices, and he shall have Power to grant Reprieves and Pardons for Offences against the United States, except in Cases of Impeachment.

He shall have Power, by and with the Advice and Consent of the Senate, to make Treaties, provided two thirds of the Senators present concur; and he shall nominate, and by and with the Advice and Consent of the Senate, shall appoint Ambassadors, other public Ministers and Consuls, Judges of the supreme Court, and all other Officers of the United States, whose Appointments are not herein otherwise provided for, and which shall be established by Law: but the Congress may by Law vest the Appointment of such inferior Officers, as they think proper, in the President alone, in the Courts of Law, or in the Heads of Departments.

The President shall have Power to fill up all Vacancies that may happen during the Recess of the Senate, by granting Commissions which shall expire at the End of their next Session.

Section. 3.

He shall from time to time give to the Congress Information of the State of the Union, and recommend to their Consideration such Measures as he shall judge necessary and expedient; he may, on extraordinary Occasions, convene both Houses, or either of them, and in Case of Disagreement between them, with Respect to the Time of Adjournment, he may adjourn them to such Time as he shall think proper; he shall receive Ambassadors and other public Ministers; he shall take Care that the Laws be faithfully executed, and shall Commission all the Officers of the United States.

Section. 4.

The President, Vice President, and all civil Officers of the United States, shall be removed from Office on Impeachment for, and Conviction of, Treason, Bribery, or other high Crimes and Misdemeanors.

ARTICLE. III.

Section. 1.

The judicial Power of the United States shall be vested in one supreme Court, and in such inferior Courts as the Congress may from time to time ordain and establish. The Judges, both of the supreme and inferior Courts, shall hold their Offices during good Behavior, and shall, at stated Times, receive for their Services, a Compensation, which shall not be diminished during their Continuance in Office.

Section. 2.

The judicial Power shall extend to all Cases, in Law and Equity, arising under this Constitution, the Laws of the United States, and Treaties made, or which shall be made, under their Authority;—to all Cases affecting Ambassadors, other public Ministers and Consuls;—to all Cases of admiralty and maritime Jurisdiction;—to Controversies to which the United States shall be a Party;—to Controversies between two or more States;— between a State and Citizens of another State,—between Citizens of different States,—between Citizens of the same State claiming Lands under Grants of different States, and between a State, or the Citizens thereof, and foreign States, Citizens or Subjects.

In all Cases affecting Ambassadors, other public Ministers, and Consuls, and those in which a State shall be Party, the supreme Court shall have original Jurisdiction. In all the other Cases before mentioned, the supreme Court shall have appellate Jurisdiction, both as to Law and Fact, with such Exceptions, and under such Regulations as the Congress shall make.

The Trial of all Crimes, except in Cases of Impeachment, shall be by Jury; and such Trial shall be held in the State where the said Crimes shall have been committed; but when not committed within any State, the Trial shall be at such Place or Places as the Congress may by Law have directed.

Section. 3.

Treason against the United States shall consist only in levying War against them, or in adhering to their Enemies, giving them Aid and Comfort. No Person shall be convicted of Treason unless on the Testimony of two Witnesses to the same overt Act, or on Confession in open Court.

The Congress shall have Power to declare the Punishment of Treason, but no Attainder of Treason shall work Corruption of Blood, or Forfeiture except during the Life of the Person attainted.

ARTICLE. IV.

Section. 1.

Full Faith and Credit shall be given in each State to the public Acts, Records, and judicial Proceedings of every other State. And the Congress may by general Laws prescribe the Manner in which such Acts, Records and Proceedings shall be proved, and the Effect thereof.

Section. 2.

The Citizens of each State shall be entitled to all Privileges and Immunities of Citizens in the several States.

A Person charged in any State with Treason, Felony, or other Crime, who shall flee from Justice, and be found in another State, shall on Demand of the executive Authority of the State from which he fled, be delivered up, to be removed to the State having Jurisdiction of the Crime.

No Person held to Service or Labour in one State, under the Laws thereof, escaping into another, shall, in Consequence of any Law or Regulation therein, be discharged from such Service or Labour, but shall be delivered up on Claim of the Party to whom such Service or Labour may be due.

Section. 3.

New States may be admitted by the Congress into this Union; but no new State shall be formed or erected within the Jurisdiction of any other State; nor any State be formed by the Junction of two or more States, or Parts of States, without the Consent of the Legislatures of the States concerned as well as of the Congress.

The Congress shall have Power to dispose of and make all needful Rules and Regulations respecting the Territory or other Property belonging to the United States; and nothing in this Constitution shall be so construed as to Prejudice any Claims of the United States, or of any particular State.

Section. 4.

The United States shall guarantee to every State in this Union a Republican Form of Government and shall protect each of them against Invasion; and on Application of the Legislature, or of the Executive (when the Legislature cannot be convened) against domestic Violence.

ARTICLE. V.

The Congress, whenever two thirds of both Houses shall deem it necessary, shall propose

Amendments to this Constitution, or, on the Application of the Legislatures of two thirds of the several States, shall call a Convention for proposing Amendments, which, in either Case, shall be valid to all Intents and Purposes, as Part of this Constitution, when ratified by the Legislatures of three fourths of the several States, or by Conventions in three fourths thereof, as the one or the other Mode of Ratification may be proposed by the Congress; Provided that no Amendment which may be made prior to the Year One thousand eight hundred and eight shall in any Manner affect the first and fourth Clauses in the Ninth Section of the first Article; and that no State, without its Consent, shall be deprived of its equal Suffrage in the Senate.

ARTICLE. VI.

All Debts contracted and Engagements entered into, before the Adoption of this Constitution, shall be as valid against the United States under this Constitution, as under the Confederation.

This Constitution, and the Laws of the United States which shall be made in Pursuance thereof; and all Treaties made, or which shall be made, under the Authority of the United States, shall be the supreme Law of the Land; and the Judges in every State shall be bound thereby, any Thing in the

Constitution or Laws of any State to the Contrary notwithstanding.

The Senators and Representatives before mentioned, and the Members of the several State Legislatures, and all executive and judicial Officers, both of the United States and of the several States, shall be bound by Oath or Affirmation, to support this Constitution; but no religious Test shall ever be required as a Qualification to any Office or public Trust under the United States.

ARTICLE. VII.

The Ratification of the Conventions of nine States shall be sufficient for the Establishment of this Constitution between the States so ratifying the Same.

The Word, "the," being interlined between the seventh and eighth Lines of the first Page, The Word "Thirty" being partly written on an Erasure in the fifteenth Line of the first Page, The Words "is tried" being interlined between the thirty second and thirty third Lines of the first Page and the Word "the" being interlined between the forty third and forty fourth Lines of the second Page.

Attest William Jackson Secretary

done in Convention by the Unanimous Consent of the States present the Seventeenth Day of September in the Year of our Lord one thou-

sand seven hundred and eighty-seven and of the
Independence of the United States of America the
Twelfth In witness whereof We have hereunto sub-
scribed our Names,

G. Washington
President and deputy from Virginia

Delaware
Geo: Read
Gunning Bedford Jun
John Dickinson
Richard Bassett
Jaco: Broom

Maryland
James McHenry
Dan of St Thos. Jenifer
Danl. Carroll

Virginia
John Blair
James Madison Jr.

North Carolina
Wm. Blount
Richd. Dobbs Spaight
Hu Williamson

South Carolina
J. Rutledge
Charles Cotesworth Pinckney
Charles Pinckney
Pierce Butler

Georgia
William Few
Abr Baldwin

New Hampshire
John Langdon
Nicholas Gilman

Massachusetts
Nathaniel Gorham
Rufus King

Connecticut
Wm. Samuel. Johnson
Roger Sherman

New York
Alexander Hamilton

New Jersey
Wil: Livingston
David Brearley
Wm. Paterson
Jona: Dayton

Pennsylvania
B Franklin
Thomas Mifflin
Robt. Morris
Geo. Clymer
Thos. FitzSimons
Jared Ingersoll
James Wilson
Gouv Morris

The Bill of Rights

Constitutional Amendments 1-10 make up what is known as The Bill of Rights. Amendments 11-27 are listed below.

AMENDMENT XI

*Passed by Congress March 4, 1794.
Ratified February 7, 1795.*

Note: Article III, section 2, of the Constitution was modified by amendment 11. The Judicial power of the United States shall not be construed to extend to any suit in law or equity, commenced or prosecuted against one of the United States by Citizens of another State, or by Citizens or Subjects of any Foreign State.

AMENDMENT XII

Passed by Congress December 9, 1803. Ratified June 15, 1804.

Note: A portion of Article II, section 1 of the Constitution was superseded by the 12th amendment. The Electors shall meet in their respective states and vote by ballot for President and Vice-President, one of whom, at least, shall not be an inhabitant of the same state with themselves; they shall name in their ballots the person voted for as President, and in distinct ballots the person voted for as Vice-President, and they shall make distinct lists of all persons voted for as President, and of all persons voted for as Vice-President, and of the number of votes for each, which lists they shall sign and certify, and transmit sealed to the seat of the government of the United States, directed to the President of the Senate; -- the President of the Senate shall, in the presence of the Senate and House of Representatives, open all the certificates and the votes shall then be counted; -- The person having the greatest number of votes for President, shall be the President, if such number be a majority of the whole number of Electors appointed; and if no person have such majority, then from the persons having the highest numbers not exceeding three on the list of those voted for as President, the House of Representatives shall choose immediately, by ballot, the President. But in choosing the President, the votes shall be taken by states, the representation from each state having one vote; a quorum for this purpose shall consist of a member or members from two-thirds of the states, and a majority of all the states shall be necessary to a choice. [And if the House of Representatives shall not choose a President whenever the right of choice shall devolve upon them, before the fourth day of March next following, then the Vice-President shall act as President, as in case of the death or other constitutional disability of the President. --]* The person having the greatest number of votes as Vice-President, shall be the Vice-President, if such number be a majority of the whole number of Electors appointed, and if no person have a majority, then from the two highest numbers on the list, the Senate shall choose the Vice-President; a quorum for the purpose shall consist of two-thirds of the whole number of Senators, and a majority of the whole number shall be necessary to a choice. But no person constitutionally ineligible to the office of President shall be eligible to that of Vice-President of the United States. *Superseded by section 3 of the 20th amendment.

AMENDMENT XIII

*Passed by Congress January 31, 1865.
Ratified December 6, 1865.*

Note: A portion of Article IV, section 2, of the Constitution was superseded by the 13th amendment.

Section 1.

Neither slavery nor involuntary servitude, except as a punishment for crime whereof the party shall have been duly convicted, shall exist within the United States, or any place subject to their jurisdiction.

Section 2.

Congress shall have power to enforce this article by appropriate legislation.

AMENDMENT XIV

*Passed by Congress June 13, 1866.
Ratified July 9, 1868.*

Note: Article I, section 2, of the Constitution was modified by section 2 of the 14th amendment.

Section 1.

All persons born or naturalized in the United States, and subject to the jurisdiction thereof, are citizens of the United States and of the State wherein they reside. No State shall make or enforce any law which shall abridge the privileges or immunities of citizens of the United States; nor shall any State deprive any person of life, liberty, or property, without due process of law; nor deny to any person within its jurisdiction the equal protection of the laws.

Section 2.

Representatives shall be apportioned among the several States according to their respective numbers, counting the whole number of persons in each State, excluding Indians not taxed. But when the right to vote at any election for the choice of electors for President and Vice-President of the United States, Representatives in Congress, the Executive and Judicial officers of a State, or the members of the Legislature thereof, is denied to any of the male inhabitants of such State, being twenty-one years of age,* and citizens of the United States, or in any way abridged, except for participation in rebellion, or other crime, the basis of representation therein shall be reduced in the proportion which the number of such male citizens shall bear to the whole number of male citizens twenty-one years of age in such State.

Section 3.

No person shall be a Senator or Representative in Congress, or elector of President and Vice-President, or hold any office, civil or military, under the United States, or under any State, who, having previously taken an oath, as a member of Congress, or as an officer of the United States, or as a member of any State legislature, or as an executive or judicial officer of any State, to support the Constitution of the United States, shall have engaged in insurrection or rebellion against the same, or given aid or comfort to the enemies thereof. But Congress may by a vote of two-thirds of each House, remove such disability.

Section 4.

The validity of the public debt of the United States, authorized by law, including debts incurred for payment of pensions and bounties for services in suppressing insurrection or rebellion, shall not be questioned. But neither the United States nor any State shall assume or pay any debt or obligation incurred in aid of insurrection or rebellion against the United States, or any claim for the loss or emancipation of any slave; but all such debts, obligations and claims shall be held illegal and void.

Section 5.

Congress shall have the power to enforce, by appropriate legislation, the provisions of this article. *Changed by section 1 of the 26th amendment.*

AMENDMENT XV

Passed by Congress February 26, 1869. Ratified February 3, 1870.

Section 1.

The right of citizens of the United States to vote shall not be denied or abridged by the United States or by any State on account of race, color, or previous condition of servitude--

Section 2.

The Congress shall have the power to enforce this article by appropriate legislation.

AMENDMENT XVI

Passed by Congress July 2, 1909. Ratified February 3, 1913.

Note: Article I, section 9, of the Constitution was modified by amendment 16.

The Congress shall have power to lay and collect taxes on incomes, from whatever source derived, without apportionment among the several States, and without regard to any census or enumeration.

AMENDMENT XVII

Passed by Congress May 13, 1912.
Ratified April 8, 1913.

Note: Article I, section 3, of the Constitution was modified by the 17th amendment.

The Senate of the United States shall be composed of two Senators from each State, elected by the people thereof, for six years; and each Senator shall have one vote. The electors in each State shall have the qualifications requisite for electors of the most numerous branches of the State legislatures.

When vacancies happen in the representation of any State in the Senate, the executive authority of such State shall issue writs of election to fill such vacancies: Provided, That the legislature of any State may empower the executive thereof to make temporary appointments until the people fill the vacancies by election as the legislature may direct.

This amendment shall not be so construed as to affect the election or term of any Senator chosen before it becomes valid as part of the Constitution.

AMENDMENT XVIII

Passed by Congress December 18, 1917. Ratified January 16, 1919. Repealed by amendment 21.

Section 1.

After one year from the ratification of this article the manufacture, sale, or transportation of intoxicating liquors within, the importation thereof into, or the exportation thereof from the United States and all territory subject to the jurisdiction thereof for beverage purposes is hereby prohibited.

Section 2.

The Congress and the several States shall have concurrent power to enforce this article by appropriate legislation.

Section 3.

This article shall be inoperative unless it shall have been ratified as an amendment to the

Constitution by the legislatures of the several States, as provided in the Constitution, within seven years from the date of the submission hereof to the States by the Congress.

AMENDMENT XIX

Passed by Congress June 4, 1919.
Ratified August 18, 1920.

The right of citizens of the United States to vote shall not be denied or abridged by the United States or by any State on account of sex.

Congress shall have power to enforce this article by appropriate legislation.

AMENDMENT XX

Passed by Congress March 2, 1932.
Ratified January 23, 1933.

Note: Article I, section 4, of the Constitution was modified by section 2 of this amendment. In addition, a portion of the 12th amendment was superseded by section 3.

Section 1.

The terms of the President and the Vice President shall end at noon on the 20th day of January, and the terms of Senators and Representatives at noon on the 3d day of January, of the years in which such terms would have ended if this article had not been ratified; and the terms of their successors shall then begin.

Section 2.

The Congress shall assemble at least once in every year, and such meeting shall begin at noon on the 3d day of January, unless they shall by law appoint a different day.

Section 3.

If, at the time fixed for the beginning of the term of the President, the President elect shall have died, the Vice President elect shall become President. If a President shall not have been chosen before the time fixed for the beginning of his term, or if the President elect shall have failed to qualify, then the Vice President elect shall act as President until a President shall have qualified; and the Congress may by law provide for the case wherein neither a President elect nor a Vice President elect shall have qualified, declaring who shall then act as President, or the manner in which one who is to act shall be selected, and such person shall act accordingly until a President or Vice President shall have qualified.

Section 4.

The Congress may by law provide for the case of the death of any of the persons from whom the House of Representatives may choose a President whenever the right of choice shall have devolved upon them, and for the case of the death of any of the persons from whom the Senate may choose a Vice President whenever the right of choice shall have devolved upon them.

Section 5.

Sections 1 and 2 shall take effect on the 15th day of October following the ratification of this article.

Section 6.

This article shall be inoperative unless it shall have been ratified as an amendment to the Constitution by the legislatures of three-fourths of the several States within seven years from the date of its submission.

AMENDMENT XXI

Passed by Congress February 20, 1933. Ratified December 5, 1933.

Section 1.

The eighteenth article of amendment to the Constitution of the United States is hereby repealed.

Section 2.

The transportation or importation into any State, Territory, or possession of the United States for delivery or use therein of intoxicating liquors, in violation of the laws thereof, is hereby prohibited.

Section 3.

This article shall be inoperative unless it shall have been ratified as an amendment to the Constitution by conventions in the several States, as provided in the Constitution, within seven years from the date of the submission hereof to the States by the Congress.

AMENDMENT XXII

Passed by Congress March 21, 1947.
Ratified February 27, 1951.

Section 1.

No person shall be elected to the office of the President more than twice, and no person who has held the office of President, or acted as President, for more than two years of a term to which some other person was elected President shall be elected to the office of the President more than once. But this Article shall not apply to any person holding the office of President when this Article was proposed by the Congress and shall not prevent any person who may be holding the office of President, or acting as President, during the term within which this Article becomes operative from holding the office of President or acting as President during the remainder of such term.

Section 2.

This article shall be inoperative unless it shall have been ratified as an amendment to the Constitution by the legislatures of three-fourths of the several States within seven years from the date of its submission to the States by the Congress.

AMENDMENT XXIII

*Passed by Congress June 16, 1960.
Ratified March 29, 1961.*

Section 1.

The District constituting the seat of Government of the United States shall appoint in such manner as the Congress may direct:

A number of electors of President and Vice President equal to the whole number of Senators and Representatives in Congress to which the District would be entitled if it were a State, but in no event more than the least populous State; they shall be in addition to those appointed by the States, but they shall be considered, for the purposes of the election of President and Vice President, to be electors appointed by a State; and they shall meet in the District and perform such duties as provided by the twelfth article of amendment.

Section 2.

The Congress shall have power to enforce this article by appropriate legislation.

AMENDMENT XXIV

*Passed by Congress August 27, 1962.
Ratified January 23, 1964.*

Section 1.

The right of citizens of the United States to vote in any primary or other election for President or Vice President, for electors for President or Vice President, or for Senator or Representative in Congress, shall not be denied or abridged by the United States or any State by reason of failure to pay any poll tax or other tax.

Section 2.

The Congress shall have power to enforce this article by appropriate legislation.

AMENDMENT XXV

*Passed by Congress July 6, 1965.
Ratified February 10, 1967.*

Note: Article II, section 1, of the Constitution was affected by the 25th amendment.

Section 1.

In case of the removal of the President from office or of his death or resignation, the Vice President shall become President.

Section 2.

Whenever there is a vacancy in the office of the Vice President, the President shall nominate a Vice President who shall take office upon confirmation by a majority vote of both Houses of Congress.

Section 3.

Whenever the President transmits to the President pro tempore of the Senate and the Speaker of the House of Representatives his written declaration that he is unable to discharge the powers and duties of his office, and until he transmits to them a written declaration to the contrary, such powers and duties shall be discharged by the Vice President as Acting President.

Section 4.

Whenever the Vice President and a majority of either the principal officers of the executive departments or of such other body as Congress may by law provide, transmit to the President pro tempore of the Senate and the Speaker of the House of Representatives their written declaration that the President is unable to discharge the powers and duties of his office, the Vice President shall immediately assume the powers and duties of the office as Acting President.

Thereafter, when the President transmits to the President pro tempore of the Senate and the Speaker of the House of Representatives his written declaration that no inability exists, he shall resume the powers and duties of his office unless the Vice President and a majority of either the principal officers of the executive department or of such other body as Congress may by law provide, transmit within four days to the President pro tempore of the Senate and the Speaker of the House of Representatives their written declaration that the President is unable to discharge the powers and duties of his office. Thereupon Congress shall decide the issue, assembling within forty-eight hours for that purpose if not in session. If the Congress, within twenty-one days after receipt of the latter written declaration, or, if Congress is not in session, within twenty-one days after Congress is required to assemble, determines by two-thirds vote of both Houses that the President is unable to discharge the powers and duties of his office, the Vice President shall continue to discharge the same as Acting President; otherwise, the President shall resume the powers and duties of his office.

AMENDMENT XXVI

Passed by Congress March 23, 1971. Ratified July 1, 1971.

Note: Amendment 14, section 2, of the Constitution was modified by section 1 of the 26th amendment.

Section 1.

The right of citizens of the United States, who are eighteen years of age or older, to vote shall not be denied or abridged by the United States or by any State on account of age.

Section 2.

The Congress shall have power to enforce this article by appropriate legislation.

AMENDMENT XXVII

Originally proposed Sept. 25, 1789. Ratified May 7, 1992.

No law, varying the compensation for the services of the Senators and Representatives, shall take effect, until an election of Representatives shall have intervened.

Regressive History

Our founding fathers had the wisdom and insight to create a constitutional republic designed to Protect liberty and freedom from tyranny... They also warned us that our freedom and liberty would have to be constantly and diligently guarded, protected, and preserved...

No nation ever created has ever experienced as much prosperity and opportunity for all its citizens... And no nation's prosperity has ever been as beneficial to all the nations on earth...

All nations have done some bad to one degree or another... But the United States of America has done better and been better for the world than any nation that has ever existed... When you know and understand that truth, it will set you free...

It's been a long, slow, relentless march for the regressives in their attempt to destroy this constitutional republic and its founding principles...

The best answer to why is there is evil in this world and in the hearts of many people and the greatest threat to that is good...

Seventy percent of America is center right... Ten percent is center left... Twenty percent is left... Of that twenty percent, only half is Marxist left... So, we have the narrative of American politics controlled by ten percent of the population...

This is due to two things... The nature of conservatism and the nature of liberalism... The nature of conservatism is to mind your own business... And the nature of liberalism is to mind everyone else's business constantly and relentlessly and slowly, patiently, in ever so tiny unnoticeable increments take away liberty and freedom...

The ultimate goal of liberalism is tyranny, and that can only be achieved when there is no liberty and freedom...

Because of the majority of Americans not being more consistent and diligent in protecting liberty, freedom, and our founding principles, the left has us approaching a point where we have regressed back to the tyranny that caused our first revolution... Only this time, it is worse because the tyranny is entrenched and from within...

But make no mistake; the majority in America will not be ruled by tyranny, and in many forms, this will be accomplished by revolt... The spirit of the American people will not be denied...

It is important to understand how we have reached this point in the United States of America, so I will herein explain the timeline of regressive events that have led us to where we are...

*****

At the very core of the problems, what we need to solve is senseless greed...

The world is not a better place when the have-nots are enslaved by the haves... In lieu of the opportunity to do great good in the world with the strength of hundreds of billions of dollars, the global banking apparatus falls victim itself to the madness of wealth and power...

In 1773, Amschel Mayor Rothschild said, "Give me control of a nation's money, and I care not who makes the laws..." In 1815, his son Nathan Rothschild said, "I care not what puppet is placed on the throne of England to rule the empire... The man that controls Brittain's money supply controls the empire... And I control the money supply..."

In 1782, the Bank of North America was founded by Robert Morris... It was given a twenty-year charter...

In 1798, Robert Morris was imprisoned for fraud and abuse... In, 1802 that charter expired...

In 1791, the first bank of the United States was established... That twenty-year charter was opposed by Alexander Hamilton, and its renewal was defeated in 1811...

Consequently, global bankers manipulated us into the war of 1812... Wars are profitable for the money controllers and expensive for the economies of nations... This war was fought so corrupt global bankers could force us to accept another bank charter... The war of 1812 lasted until 1815...because of debt pressure in 1816 the second bank of the United States was chartered for twenty years... In 1832, Andrew Jackson swore to veto a renewal of that charter... In 1835, there was an assassination attempt on the life of Andrew Jackson... In 1836, that bank charter expired...

In 1848, Karl Marx published *The Communist Manifesto*... The fifth plank of *The Communist Manifesto* is to "take over the central bank..."

(To understand the tactics of the regressives, you should study in depth the ten planks of communism, Saul Alinsky's *Rules for Radicals*, and the Cloward-Piven strategy overwhelming the welfare system and collapsing the economy to force a nation to accept socialism...)

In 1861, in order to finance the civil war, we printed demand notes, and in 1862, the Hazard Circular was published in England... It called for the need that "capital shall control labor..." This publication stated that "if that mischievous financial policy which had its origin in the North America republic should become indurated down to a fixture, then that government will furnish its own money without cost. It will pay off its debts and be without debt. It will become prosperous beyond precedent in the history of the civilized governments of the world. The brains and wealth of all countries will go to North America. That government must be destroyed, or it will destroy every monarchy on the globe."

This gets straight to the core of why innocent young people grow up wanting to "change the world..." More on that as you turn the pages...

As a direct result of the "global banking" financial pressure in 1863, the National Banking Act was given a twenty-year charter. It forced the issuing of national bank notes...

In 1864, Lincoln spoke against money power:

> I see in the near future a crisis approaching. It unnerves me and causes me to tremble for the safety of my country. The money power preys upon the nation in times of peace and conspires against it in times of adversity. It is more despotic than a monarchy, more insolent than autocracy, more selfish than bureaucracy. It denounces as public enemies all who question its method or throw light upon its crimes.
>
> I have two great enemies, the southern army in front of me and the financial institutions at the rear; The

latter is my greatest foe. Corporations
have been enthroned and an era of
corruption in high places will follow,
and the money power of the country
will endeavor to prolong its reign by
working upon the prejudices of the
people until the wealth is aggregated
in the hands of a few and the republic is destroyed.

Five months later, Lincoln was assassinated...
The national banking charter was set to expire
in 1882... President Garfield opposed its renewal...
In 1881, Garfield was assassinated...

In 1882, the national banking act was renewed
with a twenty-year charter by Andrew Johnson...

That charter was set to expire in 1902... President
McKinley opposed its renewal...

In 1901, McKinley was assassinated...

In 1902, the National Banking Act was renewed
with a twenty-year charter by Teddy Roosevelt (he
was a member of a very rich banking family) ...

The 1912 presidential election, with a very
bad economy, should have been a likely victory
for Howard Taft... But to purposely skew the election, Teddy Roosevelt, who had previously been a
Republican (in name only), ran as an independent...
This split the conservative vote, and the extremely
regressive Democrat Woodrow Wilson won the
election...

In 1913, Woodrow Wilson instituted the income tax... This was very bad in that it set the precedent and opened the floodgates for "tax and spend" regressives... And you know what they have done with taxes, fees, permits, and fines ever since... He created the Federal Reserve... This was also very harmful... Over 18 trillion in national debt is choking the life out of our economy later... That is obvious... Not to mention the economic slavery this has created for generations and generations still yet to come... The creation of the Federal Reserve was the most destructive thing regressives have ever done to this country... After 131 years with the Federal Reserve Act, a perpetual charter was given to a central bank (the fifth plank of *The Communist Manifesto*)... The USA was fundamentally changed... It amounted to a communist takeover of the central bank... It opened the door to limitless inflation, which has devalued the dollar down to being worth less than two cents... Think about that...

The Federal Reserve Act has always been and still is unconstitutional... It is in direct violation of article 1, section 2, which requires all monies to be gold and silver... More on that as you turn the pages... The federal income tax is also unconstitutional, enabled deceptively by the central taxation (Sixteenth Amendment)... More on that as you turn the pages...

It is also not inconsequential to note that Wilson was a racist who favored segregation...

Another thing that should be noted is that regressive policies at that time landed us in WWI... Coincidence?

In 1919, the Communist Party USA was founded in Chicago...

As a direct result of regressive banking policies, our economy suffered through the Great Depression in 1929... In 1933, a regressive president, FDR (another rich banking family member), came up with the New Deal... Social security was created incorrectly by FDR... From the start, it should have been absolutely privatized... That would have insured every American could retire with three or four times more than what the government now gives us... Instead, it was created intentionally as a Ponzi scheme cookie jar that later could and has been raided, illegally stealing money from the American people... This was another very harmful, destructive regressive act in our history... More on this as you turn the pages...

In 1934, FDR signed the National Firearms Act (this was harmful and unconstitutional) ...

FDR also cut our military in 1935... He started sales taxes and labor unions... All destructive actions...

Under FDR's watch, we ended up in WWII after much typical regressive appeasement and denial until our enemies were emboldened to the point where they attacked Pearl Harbor... During that time, he placed American citizens of Japanese descent in concentration camps...

John Kennedy was a rare regressive president that loved this country and did many good things... He did many bad things often with good intentions... He also did some bad things with bad intentions... Under his watch, we ended up in the Vietnam War after the French made a mess of the situation, then fled, abandoning South Vietnam...

Much like Korea, we were there to protect the freedom of the South Vietnam people... But the regressives and their useful idiot minions here in the US turned that into an unwinnable political war... War should always be the last resort, but it should be recognized when it is necessary and only be fought to win...

JFK created affirmative action... Although this was with good intentions, its mandate for perpetual reparations amounted to perpetual White slavery...

The most harmful thing JFK did to this country was create public sector unions... That action put a devastating choke hold on government itself... This was done to buy votes for the regressive party... Public sector unions should never exist...

JFK's father, Joe Kennedy, was a rich player on Wall Street in the 1920's, amassing great wealth for the Kennedy banking family... He was a major contributor to the crash of 1929, which gave us the Great Depression (which FDR's regressive policies prolonged needlessly for over ten years) ...

So, JFK understood the threat of global banking... Like Lincoln, he was fearful of the plot to enslave the American people... In the fall of 1963, he wrote,

> The very word *secrecy* is repugnant, in a free and open society, and we are as a people, inherently. and historically, opposed to secret societies, secret oaths, and to secret proceedings. But we are opposed around the world, by a monolithic and ruthless conspiracy, that relies primarily on cover means for expanding its sphere of influence, on infiltration, instead of invasion. On subversion, instead of elections. On intimidation instead of free choice.
>
> It is a system that has conscripted, vast human and material resources, into the building of a tightly Knit, highly efficient machine, that combines military, diplomatic, intelligence, economic, scientific, and political operations.
>
> Its preparations are concealed, not published. Its mistakes are buried, not headlined. Its dissenters silenced, not praised.

No expenditure is questioned. No secret is revealed.

That is why the Athenian law maker Solo declared it a crime to any citizen to shrink from controversy. I am asking for your help in the tremendous task of informing and alerting the American people. Confident with your help man will be what he was born to be, free and independent.

He endeavored to oppose global-banking tyranny...

Shortly thereafter, he was assassinated...

Next came a very harmful regressive, LBJ... He did many destructive things to America... The list of devious, deceptive, intentional damage done by this man goes on and on...

Under the guise of the "Great Society," he created Medicare and Medicaid incorrectly, having them instituted under government control instead of privatized (more cookie-jar money for corrupt government officials) ... Under the guise of "War on Poverty," he instituted the food stamp program... He began infusing federal money into the education system to entrench federal control over education... In 1967, he created the public broadcasting system to entrench federal control over the media... In 1968, he signed the Gun Control Act, which, by its very nature, violates by infringement the mandate of our constitutional rights under the Second Amendment...

During the Vietnam War, he embezzled hundreds of millions of dollars from the social security funds to pay for the war so his budget numbers would "look better..." This put strain on the social security system and has compounded ever since...

This president was the communists' and global bankers' dream...

Then Jimmy Carter came along in the seventies, and things got much, much worse...

Carter created the departments of energy and education, entrenching regressive government control... He created the environmental protection agency so regressive environmental policies could legislate by regulation... These acts were extremely harmful to freedom, liberty, and prosperity... He began the practice of auto bailouts... He reduced our military, putting our national security at risk... He gave away our Panama Canal for no good reason... He allowed Pakistan to acquire nuclear weapons...

He emboldened and encouraged Iran to take fifty-two Americans hostage for 444 days...

He plunged America into a deep recession...

Twenty years later, Bill Clinton came along and contributed his regressive damage...

He started taxing social security... He allowed North Korea to acquire nuclear weapons... He let Osama bin Ladin get away with attack after attack until the terrorists were encouraged to the point of the 9/11 attacks... He tried to implement Hillarycare (socialized medicine) ...

Clinton's worst damage was signing the affordable housing act... That created the housing-market bubble that was the main catalyst of the recession that came in 2008... It enabled and mandated predatory lending in the housing sector...

In 1994, Clinton signed the "assault" weapons ban... In 1995, he signed the Gun-Free School Zones Act... He turned our military bases into gun-free zones...

He was also neck-deep in economic and sexual scandals...

And then along came Barack Obama... He is the worst of all because of his lawless, unconstitutional approach to deliberately do harm to and inflict damage on this nation... His list of scandals is long: Operation Fast and Furious, the seizing of phone records of members of the associated press, Benghazi (where he was smuggling weapons to help create ISIS), the releasing of enemies from Guantanamo, stimulus money given to political allies, his using the IRS to target his political opponents, his using the NSA to spy on the American people, the veterans administration's neglect of veterans, Spygate (where he weaponized the DOJ, FBI, CIA, and other agencies to target political opponents in a coup attempt to overthrow an election), and many more...

He decimated our military... He has raided our national treasury, spending more than anyone ever and placing countless generations in jeopardy of destitution...

He did an illegal auto bailout where he stole ownership from investors and gave it to auto workers unions...

Through deception and lies, he passed Obamacare (socialized medicine) against the will of the majority of the American people... I don't think he did anything that wasn't against the will of the majority of the American people...

He stole over half a billion dollars from social security to implement Obamacare...

He tried to enable Iran to have nuclear weapons... Iran is the craziest of all the thin-skinned homicidal-maniac Muslim countries...

He enables millions of illegal aliens to invade our sovereignty...

He has enabled and assisted Muslim extremists throughout the Middle East and here in America... all the while doing all he can against Christians and Jews...

He exacerbated racism and set race relations back sixty years... He relentlessly attacked the Second Amendment, trying to take away everyone's guns...

To understand Obama, just research his Muslim communist past and upbringing...

*****

That is a basic chronology of the regressive history of our great nation... As you can see, there have been relentless attacks for over two hundred years...

There seems to be self-evident recurring themes in everything to do with regressive and global-banking policy... We end up in wars with both, and anyone in powerful positions who tries to shed light on the evil and oppose it gets assassinated...

We are now at a point where the things to fix are imperative...

Correcting Issues

The following solutions will restore this nation to its founding principles and improve on those principles by ensuring that they cannot be lost to destruction from within.

The beginning should be an article 5 convention of states and then lots more is needed.

These solutions can be added to or improved as necessary.

After over 200 years of economic subjugation by global bean counters and over 100 years of regressive perversion using our freedom and liberty to destroy our freedom and liberty objection will not be listened to or allowed.

Bean counters and regressives can cry all they want but to no avail because their days of ruining the greatest nation ever created are over...

*The Federal Reserve will be abolished. We will return to article I section II of the Constitution and return to the gold and silver standard.

The scam of global bean counters subjugating the masses has been in play and refined since civilization began.

In 1862 there was a publication in The London Times called the hazard circular...

It directly addresses the bottom line and fundamental reason why generation after generation of young people feel the need to "change the world" ... Human existence is rigged.

Unless you're one of the rich your enslaved to serve the rich with little hope of rising up out of the mud. Young people can see and sense this and innocently know it is not right.

The hazard circular was written by global bean counters concerned that the USA might threaten and do away with the enslavement of the have nots. The singular goal of the global bean counters is to make sure capital controls labor.

Once again, the hazard circular reads as follows:

"If the mischievous financial policy which had its origin in North America republic should become indurate down to a fixture, then that government will furnish its own money without debt. It will pay off its debts and be without debt. It will become prosperous beyond president in the history of civilized governments of the world. The brains and wealth of all countries will go to North America. That government must be destroyed, or it will destroy every monarchy on the globe..."

So, the end result is the world will finally have the change it needs. And the example it sets will be such a sharp and compelling contrast to that rest of the world will want to come to the USA or achieve the same condition where they are.

This change will be higher than the Magne Carta and the Declaration of Independence.

Unprecedented liberty, freedom, economic opportunity, and the real pursuit of happiness will be a beacon to all of humanity.

This will immediately release the death grip the global bean counters have on the American people and the American economy.

Since its creation the Federal Reserve has caused a hidden tax that is by far the worst tax of all. It has caused inflation.

The United States Treasury on the gold standard can, when necessary, borrow from itself interest free instead of making global bean counters richer off the backs of hard-working Americans.

*The IRS will be eliminated and replaced by a simple flat tax for individuals, companies, and corporations. This will attract companies to operate in the USA and people will have more of their own money to spend as they wish. This will take over 74,000 tax pages of tax code down to a few pages and will greatly reduce the size of the government.

*There will be a balanced budget amendment. No spending of money we don't have will be allowed.

* The national debt will be paid off. This will be easily accomplished by several of the solutions implemented here...

*Foreign aid will be reduced and all foreign aid to countries that are not our allies will be eliminated...

*The United States will no longer be a member of the United Nations. The United Nations has become nothing but a group of deceitful regressives working for bean counters. We will no longer be part of that deceit. The United Nations will be kicked out of the USA, and we will not give them any of our money.

* Foreign ownership of U.S. property and companies will be illegal and strictly enforced. The USA is not for sale.

* Foreign contributions to U.S. elections, elected officials, and any U.S. organizations will be illegal and strictly enforced.

*Election Fraud and cheating will be illegal and strictly enforced. Anyone caught in any form of election fraud will lose their citizenship and be deported after proper punishment. This will include anyone that writes code in voting machines that switches votes from the actual vote to someone else.

* Laws will be established that prohibit the rich and corporations from influencing the government. No lobbying will be allowed, and no pork barrel spending projects will be allowed to be attached to any legislation. Also, if you don't pay taxes and

show I.D. you don't vote. These protections will be strictly enforced.

* Anyone caught giving money or any other form of enrichment to anyone in government, and anyone in government caught accepting money or any other form of enrichment will lose their citizenship and be deported after proper punishment.

*Anyone in government or government agencies caught legislating or ruling by mandate to profit themselves, their families, their relatives, or associates will lose their citizenship and be deported after proper punishment.

*Any legislation affecting more than 5% of the economy will require a 2/3rds majority vote of the people (not congress).

* Everyone in government and government agencies will be subject to all legislation and mandated rules implemented by government and government agencies.

* The Federal government will not be in control of more than 5% of state lands. Public lands shall be under the administration of the state. The BLM will be eliminated.

*The good of the people and humans will have final priority over unneeded environmental concerns. The EPA will be under the administration of the states and will not have regulatory authority without representation.

* Term limits will apply to all elected offices and branches of the Federal government. (8 Years

for President 12 years for court judges) If any of those positions are found to not be enforcing existing laws and upholding the constitution, they will lose their citizenship and be deported after proper punishment.

If a person is sworn into office to uphold the laws and the constitution and then does not do so, they will be removed from office. "The constitution says what it says and doesn't say what it doesn't say" … Supreme Court Justice Antonin Scalia

*Clarification will be added to the 14th Amendment to not allow anchor babies. A child born of two foreigners born in the United States will not be a United States citizen. Only two countries allow this. We will no longer be one of them.

In 1866, Senator Jacob Howard clearly spelled out the intent of the 14th Amendment by stating:

"Every person born within the limits of The United States, and subject to their jurisdiction, is by virtue of natural law and national law a citizen of The United States. This will not of course include persons born in The United States who are foreigners, aliens, who belong to the families of Ambassadors or foreign ministers accredited to Government of The United States but will include every other class of persons. It settles the great question of citizenship and removes all doubt as to what persons are or are not citizens of The United States. This has long been a great desideratum in the jurisprudence and legislation of this country."

This understanding was reaffirmed by Senator Edward Cowan, who stated: "{A foreigner in The United States} has a right to the protection of the laws, but he is not a citizen in the country in the ordinary acceptance of the word."

The phrase "subject to the jurisdiction thereof" was intended to exclude American-born persons from automatic citizenship whose allegiance to The United States was not complete. With illegal aliens who are unlawfully in The United States, their native country has a claim of allegiance on the child. Thus, the completeness of their allegiance to The United States is impaired, which therefore precludes automatic citizenship.

With the federal government reduced to its proper size we will have at least 100 billion dollars less in expenses they now call "general government".

When we implement term limits in congress and the courts and reduce needlessly enormous pensions for offices and get rid of quadruple public sector union pensions, we will save over 1 trillion dollars a year.

When we get rid of professional deadbeats and the needless part of the never-ending welfare state, we will save over 2 trillion dollars a year (and still have 1 ½ trillion dollars a year to help those who truly are in need).

No more of the scam where the regressives use the tax dollars of the makers to buy the votes of the takers.

The correct interpretation of the 14th Amendment is that an illegal alien mother is subject to the jurisdiction of her native country as is her baby.

We must also eliminate the other "incentives" that attract illegal aliens to invade our sovereignty... These include the illegal asylum scam in place by congress, sanctuary cities and states, free schooling for illegal aliens, welfare benefits for illegal aliens, catch and release (instead of catch and deport) and all other forms of enticement for aliens to invade our country. There will be no more lottery migration and no more chain migration. There will only be merit based migration.

*A fifty-foot-high wall will be built the entire length of the Mexican and Canadian borders. As much manpower and technology will be employed to make sure both borders and all ports of entry are impassable except by legal passage. All illegal aliens will be deported and go to the back of the legal immigration line. This will be far less expensive than what we are doing now with unenforced open borders and unenforced immigration policies. Not to mention our national security sovereignty.

* Long- term loans will be limited to 50% and short-term loans will be limited to 20%. In other words, global banking bean counters will no longer

be able to charge a home buyer 750,000 dollars for a 200,000-dollar loan. The amount will be 400,000 on a 200,000-dollar home.

*Federal government will be reduced and limited to only its powers and functions enumerated in the constitution. Departmental bureaucracies such as but not limited to the Dept. of Education, Dept. of Energy, Environmental Protection Agency, etc. shall be controlled by the states.

* Public sector unions will not be allowed to exist.

*Public radio and television will not be allowed to exist.

* Affirmative actions will not be allowed to exist.

*Welfare will not be allowed to exist as a career.

*Taxpayers will not be forced to pay for other people's children to go to school. If people have children, they will pay for their own children to go to school. Most countries rightly do it this way and with proper non-public sector union schools it is inexpensive and more efficient.

*There will be no taxpayer funding of planned parenthood and any other such organizations.

They can exist in the private sector or cease to exist. (And all the criminal activity in planned parenthood will be punished retroactively.)

*Social Security will be privatized and removed from the reach of government. And all the money stolen from the social security fund (by 3 different regressive presidents) will be restored with interest.

*Medicare and Medicaid will be improved with privatization and health saving accounts. All money stolen from these funds by regressives (including Obama) will be restored with interest.

*Our health care system will be restored to free market and improved with open border competition and tort reform, this will recreate patient based health care and drastically reduce the cost of health care, It will lower the cost of insurance through competition and doctors and hospitals not having to spend hundreds of thousands of dollars for malpractice insurance because lawyers are currently allowed to sue for 50 times more than what is reasonable.

* Our military will be made the best strongest and most powerful on earth.

* Our military will be allowed to have weapons on military bases.

* War is always the last resort. Wars will be fought to win, and rules of engagement will not be allowed. Anyone who tries to undermine war efforts will lose their citizenship and be deported after proper punishment.

* Regressives will be removed from our military and all patriots that have been purged for politics will be reinstated.

* Regressives, Muslims, hate groups, and career welfare deadbeats will not be allowed to exist in the United States. They will lose their citizenship and be deported. No liberals, socialists, communists,

Muslims, hate groups, and parasites that vote for a living instead of working for a living will be allowed. Liberalism, socialism, communism, Islam, hate groups, and leeches will be illegal.

We already know who they are and where they are.

They will not be allowed to take their riches, that they stole from the American people with them. They will only be allowed 30,000 dollars or 10% of their wealth (whichever is greater). The rest will go back into the National Treasury to be used to pay off the national debt.

Once they have satisfied financial and criminal obligations they will be deported as refugees to goodriddensylvania. I don't care if that is Antarctica. (Being allowed to live at all is more than they deserve).

A better way is to do an exchange with Australia.

There are 20 million people in Australia. Half are conservative living in disgust under the tyrannical governance of regressives. They can come here and be given double what their property there is worth, those that have little will be set up for success.

A minimum of 60 to 80 million regressives, Muslims, members of hate groups, and deadbeats will be sent to Australia. Takers from here will join 10 million takers in goodriddensylvania and they can have their regressive utopia. All they have to do is figure out who is going to pay for everything.

They can have politically correct, all day, every day. They can enjoy gun control, race-baiting, riots, looting, gay parades, abortions, Godless society, man caused climate change mythology, and hug all the Muslims they want.

Some of the former citizens will be retained and held accountable for crimes and wrong doings.

They will face execution or incarceration after which they will join their comrades in goodriddensylvania.

There will be instances where immediate family members will be regressive and conservative (but not too many because the two are not compatible). In those cases, appeals will be heard, but if denied due to a family member being a regressive extremist then personal choices will have to be made. Sometimes life is tough.

Those refugees in goodriddensylvania can choose to stay there or seek asylum anywhere else in the world that will except them.

It will be illegal to lie to American people on purpose. This will include news broadcasts, documentaries, nature shows, politicians, and any and every other representation. Deception will not be allowed, and this will be strictly enforced. The lying propaganda is finished.

These solutions will effectively put an end to political correctism. They will undo damage that has needed to be undone for too many years from Wilson, FDR, Kennedy, LBJ, Carter, Clinton, Obama, (and others).

At first it may take some getting used to, especially if you were born after 1980. We have been conditioned to accept way too many forfeitures of our freedom, liberty, and moral fabric. We will have the return of the concept of "mind your own business". Neighbors will know and watch out for each other. No regressives in schools and colleges brainwashing our children with regressive rubbish. But instead, actually teaching knowledge and truth, No regressive indoctrination teaching what to think instead of how to think.

No regressives in the media peddling misinformation. No regressives in DC and on the courts shoving Marxist tyranny down our throats.

Just being able to live our lives carefree and enjoy prosperity and simple pleasures without subversive forces constantly and stealthily attacking and ruining our pursuit of happiness.

These solutions will make the human condition in the USA better than it has ever been in the entire history of mankind.

Bean counters will not have a choking grip on the American workers and the American economy.

Takers will not burden the makers. Death cult maniacs will not be in the USA. Hate based religion, race, or anything else will not be allowed.

Gun laws will be replaced because the Second Amendment says "shall not be infringed" so there will no longer be the National Fire Arms Act of 1934, The Gun Control act of 1968, the Brady and Gun Violence Act of 1993, the Assault Weapons Ban of 1994, and the Gun Free School and Military Base Zones Act of 1995, our children and soldiers will be protected.

Doesn't matter how these solutions are achieved and implemented. There is no can't about it. Only can. If we have to use Article 5 of the Constitution. Or let our military go full Egypt then so be it. However else it has to be achieved then so be it.

There will be no more bank charters with treacherous global bean counters such as the charters that marred the first half of this country's existence.

Wilson's permanent subjugation to global bean counters and his income tax scam will be undone.

FDR's "New deal" will become the "gone deal".

Kennedy's affirmative action and public sector union scams will go away,

LBJ's 'great society' scam will go away,

Carter's regressive takeover of our schools, and environment, private property, and privacy will be undone.

Clinton's illegal assaults on the 2nd Amendment and the economy in favor of Wall Street bean counters will be no more.

Obama's destruction of the greatest health care system on earth will be undone and so much better actual improvements will be implemented. His illegal and harmful attacks on our economy, Christians, our military, and the fabric of our society that makes us great will be reversed forever.

Enough. That's it!

There will be bawling like branded calves "What about the Constitution and our rights?" etc. etc.

For over 100 years the rights of the American people have been violated by regressives. The Constitution has been attacked at every turn.

It's too late and way beyond the point phony regressive indignation will matter.

The passive aggressive politically correct tyranny is finished.

That's it... Get out...Good riddance forever...

Imagine a world where you get to keep 80% of what you earn instead of 45%... That will be the difference. 20% will be enough to Fund all necessary government needs. Keeping 80% will enable you to be able to afford your home, and most such basic wants without spending your life stuck in the mud of the rat race paying interest.

Imagine working hard and being able to retire comfortably at 55 or 50 when you can still enjoy your retirement instead of slaving away in perpetual debt until the day you die of old age and exhaustion.

Instead of financing billionaires to double and triple their wealth living lives of luxury from vacation to vacation while you can't afford a vacation, you get to enjoy the fruits of your own labor instead of billionaires stealing your money.

With these solutions in place the human condition in the United States will be forever changed, and the rest of the world will demand to follow.

The world will be forever changed...

The political and financial game of power and control will be over...

It will no longer be possible for the masses to be set upon and enslaved by evil connivers.

For the first time in human history young people won't have to grow up feeling that the world is not how it should be and feeling hopeless frustration to be able to "change the world" no longer will they have to "grow up" by accepting that, the world is not how it should be and that's just how it is.

How to Pay Off
the National Debt

This is my outline to have our national debt paid in full within ten to fifteen years...

The defense budget will be increased by 10 percent, and our military will be built up beyond anyone being able to challenge... We will have peace through strength...

We will have the largest best-equipped military on earth with the most advanced technology known and unknown...

All other government spending will be immediately cut by 5 percent... That will save 234 billion a year even after the 10 percent increase in the defense budget...

Plus, we will save 3.2 trillion dollars a year when we are rid of the public sector union pensions, the professional welfare deadbeats, and the federal government that will be greatly reduced to its proper size...

We will save over seventy billion a year by not giving foreign aid to countries that are not our allies... That is absolutely ridiculous and a shameful waste of taxpayer dollars...

When you combine all that with a balanced budget amendment and the money recovered from those expelled to Goodriddinsylvania, we will be a debt free nation in less than a generation...

National treasure plundered by thieves will be returned to its rightful owners...

With all that said we will still be forking out 39 billion in annual foreign aid to countries that are our allies...

With the federal government reduced to its proper size we will have at least 100 billion dollars less in expenses they now call "general government". When we implement term limits in congress and the courts and reduce needlessly enormous pensions for offices and get rid of quadruple public sector union pensions, we will save over 1 trillion dollars a year. When we get rid of professional deadbeats and the needless part of the never-ending welfare state, we will save over 2 trillion dollars a year (and still have 1 ½ trillion dollars a year to help those who truly are in need). No more of the scam, where the regressives use the tax dollars of the makers to buy the votes of the takers...

Enough

Inside the beltway, know nothing know- it -all experts will scoff at these solutions with the scorn of a Scrooge on Christmas eve.

They will lay around like Jabba the Hut with their bloated triple chins having gorged themselves on money stolen from the taxpayers. They will say "that's not who we are' and "you can't do this "and "you can't do that" But they will be wrong.

This is who we are. We can do this, we will, and we must.

The caveman Mook the moocher said "You can't invent the wheel" ... Others said "You can't invent a boat" and "You can't prove the Earth is round" and "you can't invent a plane, discover electricity, build a steam engine, a gasoline engine, or put a man on the Moon" there is never a shortage of those who say "you can't do this or that" And without planned parenthood murdering millions of babies we can have more discoveries such as curing cancer and eliminating hunger, figuring out how to harness magnetics to conquer gravity, achieve the speed of light, master the space/time continuum etc. etc.

More and more the hard-working people of America are arrogantly taken for granted by the elite regressives, and bean counters who mistakenly think of themselves as omniscient. We are being exploited to serve the interests of others.

This is being done through the most insidious form of slavery known as debt. The source of this despicable crime is the Federal Reserve, which is an entrenched tool used by the bean counters. The Federal Reserve steals from us in two ways. It creates inflation by printing money out of thin air which steals the value of our money, and it ensures that the have nots, remain have nots and are forced to borrow and have to pay countless fortunes to bean counters in interest while they wallow in their vaults on enormous piles of riches like Scrooge McDuck.

How much is enough? The more bean counter elites have the more they want... If they have 100 million they want 200 million. If they have 1 billion, they want 2 billion. Never mind the serfs and peasants... Let the huddled masses eat cake (then get back to work and feed the big pig, because in Orwellian reality some animals are more equal than others) ... Shut up and be happy donating your existence to the greed for money and power of bean counters and regressives as free-range humans controlled and manipulated in the illusion of a free society.

It does no good to play their game and try to elect patriots to go to Washington DC and try to tweak around the edges to fix what needs fixed.

They are met with entrenched opposition from regressive commies and big money bean counter lobbyist filibustering and blocking and very little or nothing can be accomplished.

It is way past the point of rescue. Bold and courageous revolutionary action is the only needed solution.

Allowing regressives and bean counters to live is more than they deserve. It is not justice for those who have died and existed in hopeless subjugation at their hands. In France, they marched them all to the guillotine. It is an act of mercy and compassion to allow them to leave as refugees. Some will stay and answer for their crimes against humanity.

The lies, deceit and evil of regressive and bean counters will be banished and forbidden.

We will run off the bean counters like Jesus confronting their predecessors in the Temple Mount.

We will rid ourselves of the cancerous vermin that eat away at the fabric of all that is good about our society and America...

We will no longer be subjugated to the tyranny of economic slavery, the insecurity of parasitic political destitution, and the terror threatened by evil.

We will have real happiness and domestic tranquility...

Imagine a world where we get to keep our own money and not be obligated to debt, where we are not collateral for the national debt. Where we work for ourselves instead of others. Where there are no regressives and bean counters with their boots on our throats. Where there are no thin-skinned homicidal maniacs living next door hating us for not being a member of their religion.

Where we don't have millions upon millions of illegal aliens and career deadbeats sucking the lifeblood out of our economy. (The rule of right will once again be applied... People will only come here legally and only live here in the concept of improving their lives through ambition and hard work, no more politically correcting, and voting others into hand feeding them for grapes as servants and slaves). Imagine a life where you can retire early if you want... where children are raised to be responsible, respectful, and moral... where those children don't think they need to change the world.

Imagine not being born poor into destitution of subjugation to a life of "interest payments."

Imagine hunger and starvation not being the consequence of enough never being enough for bean counters in their vaults.

Imagine a life without boots of regressives and bean counters on your throat. Imagine never having to worry again about our freedom and liberty being used to destroy our freedom and liberty.

Life will be as it should, and the world will be a better place.

Invictus

by William Ernest Henley

Out of the night that covers me,
Black as the pit from pole to pole,
I thank whatever gods may be
For my unconquerable soul.

In the fell clutch of circumstance
I have not winced nor cried aloud.
Under the bludgeoning's of chance
My head is bloody, but unbowed.

Beyond this place of wrath and tears
Looms but the Horror of the shade,
And yet the menace of the years
Finds, and shall find, me unafraid.

It matters not how strait the gate,
How charged with punishments the
    scroll,
I am the master of my fate:
I am the captain of my soul.

About the Author

Milan Albert is a conservative patriot who believes the true meaning of success is if the world is "a better place" because you were here...